T0079775

HERRING

Edible

Series Editor: Andrew F. Smith

EDIBLE is a revolutionary series of books dedicated to food and drink that explores the rich history of cuisine. Each book reveals the global history and culture of one type of food or beverage.

Already published

Herring

A Global History

Kathy Hunt

REAKTION BOOKS

Published by Reaktion Books Ltd
Unit 32, Waterside
44–48 Wharf Road
London N1 7UX, UK
www.reaktionbooks.co.uk

First published 2017

Copyright © Kathy Hunt 2017

All rights reserved
No part of this publication may be reproduced, stored in a retrieval
system, or transmitted, in any form or by any means, electronic,
mechanical, photocopying, recording or otherwise, without the prior
permission of the publishers

Printed and bound in China by Toppan Leefung Printing Limited

A catalogue record for this book is available from the British Library

ISBN 978 1 78023 831 9

Contents

Introduction

For centuries the small, unassuming, ocean-dwelling fish known as herring has served as the backbone for countless European and North American communities, providing sustenance and economic stability to millions. In the Viking era it fed both the Norse marauders and their conquests. During the Middle Ages it prompted the founding of fishing villages and port cities such as Great Yarmouth, Copenhagen and Amsterdam. Along with creating commonwealths, it spurred the formation of a structured workforce and fish-selling guilds. In twelfth-century France, where herring was a luxurious indulgence, herring sellers or *harengères* were deemed the crème de la crème of the fishmonger guilds.

Herring inspired the inception of maritime rights, the thought rightly being that no creature as coveted as herring could be left unregulated or unprotected. Even so, the fish still sparked raids, riots and fights. From the 1429 Battle of the Herrings between England and France to the 2013 herring war between the European Union and Faroe Islands, these skirmishes have spanned the centuries.

History teaches us that wars usually end in treaties. Herring conflicts were no exception. They produced pacts such as the

Treaty of 1818, which gave the United States permission to fish along the coast of Newfoundland and Labrador.

Founding cities, providing food and jobs, prompting wars and treaties – that's quite a list of accomplishments for a fish that maxes out at 30 cm long and 700 g. Don't applaud herring too soon, for its reach extends even further, into language and culture. Take the case of red herring. In addition to denoting a type of smoked fish, the term refers to anything serving as a diversion or deliberate misdirection.

The fish stars in such English slang as 'dead as a herring'. The former phrase dates back to the sixteenth century and alludes to the horrendous odour that a dead herring gives off, leaving its death unquestionable. It is a take on the fourteenth century's 'dead as a doornail', which also means quite dead or done.

Another English original, 'done up like a kipper', implies that a person has been framed, betrayed or caught red-handed. Most historians attribute this meaning to the actual definition of a kipper. This is a herring that has been split, gutted and hung up to smoke and dry. If framed for an act you didn't commit or left to face a horrible situation on your own, you certainly could feel that, like a kipper, you had been hung out to dry.

Sketch of Atlantic herring, *Clupea harengus*, from *Elements of Comparative Zoology* (1905).

Landscape painter Winslow Homer's *The Herring Net*, 1885.

Along with infiltrating the English language, herring have sneaked into poetry and prose. The eighteenth-century Irish writer and satirist Jonathan Swift composed the following verse about Irish herring sellers:

Be not sparing,
Leave off swearing,
Buy my Herring
Fresh from Malahide,
Better nc'cr was try'd.
Come eat 'em with pure fresh Butter and Mustard,
Their Bellies are soft and white as Custard.
Come Sixpence a Dozen to get some Bread,
Or, like my own Herrings, I soon shall be dead.

Swift wasn't the only eighteenth-century writer to feature the diminutive fish in his work. In the 1791 narrative poem 'Tam O'Shanter' the Scottish poet Robert Burns proclaims, 'Ah, Tam! ah Tam! thou'll get thy fairin'! / In hell they'll roast thee like a herrin'!' Nor was herring limited to the printed page. In 1885 the American landscape painter Winslow Homer painted *The Herring Net*, a depiction of two English fishermen hauling their glistening herring catch into their small, wooden boat. Homer's grand work now hangs in the Art Institute of Chicago. The nineteenth-century Scottish artist Robert Weir Allan portrayed herring fishermen unloading their catch in *Home from the Herring Fishing*. It is now part of the Glasgow Museums collection in Scotland. In the 1889 *Still-life with Smoked Herrings on Yellow Paper* the Dutch post-Impressionist Vincent Van Gogh showcased herring on its own. He did the same in a series of paintings of bloaters, plump, lightly salted and smoked herring.

Considering herring's tremendous impact upon and prevalence in Europe, North America and parts of Asia, you might assume that everyone in the world has heard of this rich, white-fleshed fish. This, however, is not the case. Ask the average American to name one thing he knows about herring and you will more than likely receive a blank or questioning stare in return. For the majority of stateside consumers, herring have slipped off their historical, economic and culinary radars. Overfishing, sporadic availability and a hesitancy to deviate from tried and true foods are among the reasons why herring has such a small presence in contemporary American cuisine. Fortunately, the same cannot be said about the rest of the world's fare. In such disparate locales as Japan and Belgium, herring remains a popular source of protein.

Because I grew up in a landlocked region north of Pittsburgh, Pennsylvania, where the seafood on offer consisted of cod, flounder, tuna and salmon, I was a latecomer to herring. Even then, my introduction was purely accidental. Travelling through England during graduate school, I had anticipated experiencing such quintessential British repasts as

Herring fillets, a common sight in a Scandinavian grocery store.

fish and chips, afternoon tea, sticky toffee pudding and the full English breakfast. Instead, what I encountered on my first morning in London was a stainless steel toast caddy filled with brown bread, a plate of butter, a bowl of lemon wedges and a platter covered with split, flattened, golden-hued, odoriferous fish. The glorious egg, bacon, sausage, grilled tomatoes and mushrooms of those fabled English breakfasts were nowhere to be seen.

After a few embarrassed enquiries about what to do with the food in front of me, I placed a small piece of oily fish, which I'd separated from its silvery skin, on a slice of buttered bread. I then squeezed a lemon wedge over the fish and sprinkled a smidgen of ground black pepper over top. Using my fork, I cut off a tiny portion of the open-faced sandwich and took a tentative first bite of smoked herring, or, as it's commonly called in Great Britain, kipper.

What I remember most was the delicate, creamy texture and mildly smoky, hearty taste. Much to my delight, herring turned out to be not only edible but tasty and filling. Its robust, meaty flavour called to mind sardines and shad, two other omega-3 fatty-acid-rich fish with which I'd recently become acquainted. I later learned that herring, sardines and shad belong to the same family, Clupeidae, so the similarities could be expected.

After that enjoyable, albeit unusual, meal I was smitten. Forget my desires to gorge on traditional English breakfasts and endless variations on battered and deep-fried plaice, cod or haddock. I was now on a quest for herring.

If you're in pursuit of herring, Great Britain and continental Europe provide the ideal hunting grounds. The fish maintains a strong presence there, headlining in such European specialities as rollmops, *surströmming, grüner Heringe* and, of course, kippers. In the Netherlands food carts known as *haringkar* serve fresh, young herring, or *maatjes,* as they did in the fifteenth century. In Scandinavia *sillsallad*, or herring salad, varies according to the country or kitchen you visit. In Denmark, which was one of the first countries to prosper from herring, there are purportedly twice as many pickled

Men eating herring the traditional Dutch way in the Netherlands.

Jars of pickled herring displayed in the refrigerated section of a Scandinavian market.

herring recipes as there are days of the year. Having spent considerable time in Denmark, sampling slivers of herring at markets and pavement food stalls, on *kolde bords*, the equivalent of the Swedish smorgasbord, and in upscale restaurants, I can attest to the diversity.

If you strike up conversations about herring with local fishermen, fishmongers and cooks, you're bound to pick up a few unusual stories. Among the stranger tales related to me was the notion that herring sneeze upon being pulled out of the ocean. As sceptical as I am about this claim, the late American journalist and food writer Waverley Root also mentioned sneezing herring in his 1980 encyclopaedia *Food*.

The legends don't end with a sneeze. In Belgium it is said that herring schools off the coast grow so large that they resemble an island rising from the sea or a new continent about to emerge. In Øresund, the strait between Danish

Zealand and Swedish Scania, the herring population was reputedly once so copious that people stuck their hands into the water and plucked out the fish. My favourite, though, is a Dutch aphorism advising, 'A herring a day keeps the doctor away.' And all these years I've eaten apples!

There are scientific discoveries that sound a bit like tall tales. Take for instance the 2003 National Geographic News report stating that herring use flatulence as a way of communicating. Called Fast Repetitive Ticks, or FRT, these expulsions of gas alert surrounding herring but keep predators in the dark. It's a surprisingly effective means of communication and finally a justifiable excuse for breaking wind.

To understand the popularity and power of herring, it is best to start with the fish itself. It may be petite and unpretentious but it packs a mighty nutritional and historical punch.

I

Small Fish, Big Presence

If you've ever sailed off on a whale-watching tour, you may recall the keen anticipation of seeing a majestic humpback, minke or orca whale. When you spot a moving object on the horizon, anticipation leads to excitement, quickly followed by disappointment and boredom. Instead of a whale, what you see, time and again, is a porpoise, small boat or flotsam. If you happen to be on an excursion near Washington's Puget Sound and San Juan Islands, you might be lucky enough to spy enormous schools of slender, silvery, narrow-headed fish swimming near the water's surface. Members of the Clupeidae family, to which shad, menhaden and sardines also belong, these petite, soft-finned fish are known as *Clupea pallasii*, or Pacific herring.

Geographically, Pacific herring reach as far north as the Arctic Ocean and White Sea. In the eastern North Pacific they can be found from Baja California, Mexico, to Alaska's Beaufort Sea. In the western North Pacific their territory stretches from Russia to the Yellow Sea along China and the Korean Peninsula.

In the Atlantic the similarly sized and shaped *Clupea harengus*, or Atlantic herring, inhabits the ocean's cold waters in large shoals. This fish roams the Atlantic Ocean and Baltic

Image of *Clupea pallasii,* Pacific herring.

Sea, swimming as far southwest as France and as far southeast as the Chesapeake Bay. Its biggest populations reside north of Cape Cod, Massachusetts. South of New Jersey its numbers peter out. Like its Pacific brethren, Atlantic herring may be referred to by their region: Baltic herring are from the Baltic Sea, and so on.

To complicate the nomenclature, there is also a fish known as the Atlantic spring herring or alewife. Despite resembling the herring in its shoaling patterns and gregariousness, the alewife is larger and eats other fish, including herring, shrimp and eels. Another difference is that it spawns only in streams. Of limited commercial interest today, it is either salted and sold for human consumption or used as bait for cod, haddock and pollock.

North America also has the deceptively named lake herring. Found in Lake Huron and Lake Superior, this fish is neither a herring nor a member of the Clupeidae family. Instead this small, silvery, freshwater fish belongs to the

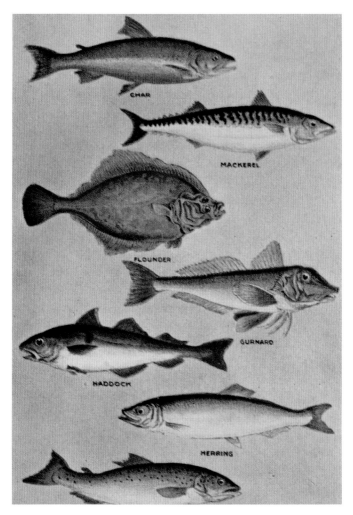

Illustrated fish chart in the American Smiley's *Cook Book and Universal Household Guide* (1895).

Salmonidae family, the same group to which salmon and trout belong.

Even within its own family, herring gets mistaken for other fish. Most often it is confused for sardines. Yet sometimes another fish, the sprat, is mislabelled as herring. This silvery, oily fish looks a bit like a herring but it is much smaller – between 9 and 12 cm (3.5 and 5 in.) long.

All herring are pelagic fish, which means that they live in open seas, away from the shoreline and the bottom of the ocean, and survive on the microorganisms in the water. Furthermore, herring are forage fish, small, vulnerable creatures that fall victim to predators such as terns, puffins, cod, salmon, porpoises, seals, whales and fishermen. Contrary to their name and to the popular belief, herring gulls generally do not hunt this fish.

Thanks to the herring's desirability, if you do spot this fish on a whale excursion, you may also come across a hungry minke whale. The minke may be stalking a peculiar swirling object known as a bait ball. When feeling threatened, forage

A lucky tern clutching a freshly caught fish.

Bait ball swirling in the Gulf of the Farallones National Marine Sanctuary off the coast of San Francisco, California.

fish instinctually huddle together, forming this gigantic yet compact orb. This is their only real defence against attackers.

According to the National Oceanic and Atmospheric Administration, roughly two hundred species of herring exist. The largest reach 45 cm (18 in.) in length and weigh slightly more than 450 g (1 lb). In the Pacific the average adult size is 25 cm (10 in.) while in the Atlantic, where herring are the most abundant, the average size is 18 cm (7 in.).

Size aside, the various species of herring share physical characteristics, including a small, single, central dorsal fin. Lacking spines, this fin is soft and short. Additionally, none of the species' pectoral fins move. This immobility prohibits sudden stopping, reverse movement or hovering in the water. The fish can only veer up and down and left and right.

Deeply forked tails allow for extended bouts of fast swimming, up to 20 knots (37 km) per hour. Tapered heads and long bodies further increase their speed in the water. These are handy attributes for fish known to travel great distances to reach their spawning grounds.

Shimmering silver in colour with hints of bluish green on their backs, herring have large, silver scales that readily come off. In *Jane Grigson's Fish Book* (1993) their scales are poetically described as deciduous 'because they fall as easily as leaves from autumn trees'. Needless to say, they make descaling a breeze.

Along with beauty, herring have been blessed with a remarkable sense of hearing. They use this complex auditory system to communicate with other herring via a method known as Fast Repetitive Ticks, FRT. Other herring can hear FRT, which is the underwater expulsion of gas, because these fish can detect frequencies up to 40,000 kHz. This makes them on par with dogs, which also pick up sounds at 40,000 kHz, and superior to humans, who can hear up to 20,000 kHz. This superb sense of hearing enables them look out for each other and themselves.

Besides sharing physical traits, all herring exhibit a sociable streak. Simply put, they like to hang out with fellow herring and other little fish. Genial creatures, they have been known to stay in the same school for their entire lives. This is especially impressive when you consider that herring can live to be nineteen years old.

Schools of herring tend to be colossal. In fact, bands covering roughly 16 square kilometres (6 square miles) and numbering approximately one billion have been sighted in the Atlantic Ocean. In 1877 off the coast of England a herring shoal measuring 32 metres, or 18 fathoms, deep was spotted. Some historians believe that these large groupings inspired the fish's English name. They attribute 'herring' to the Danish and Norwegian word for army, *haer*, which their mammoth ranks are said to resemble.

Although there is some safety in their massive numbers and tendency to form tightly packed bait balls, herring take further precautions against becoming prey. To reduce the likelihood of being seen, and eaten, by their adversaries, they feed at night. Under cover of darkness they attack and bite their quarry or they filter feed, straining sustenance from the water with their gill rakers, the bony projections sticking out of their gill arches. When fearing attacks, they keep a low profile and eat in this passive manner.

What they eat dictates when they eat. Herring consume plankton, which consists of miniscule plants known as phyto-plankton and tiny animals called zooplankton. The latter includes such diminutive crustaceans as copepods, the slightly larger krill and fish eggs and larvae. During the daylight hours these organisms stay in deep waters, but at night they drift upwards to the surface waters that herring inhabit. This makes

Tiny krill, essential to the herring's diet.

them easy pickings for the hungry fish. By eating plankton from the bottom of the food chain, herring develop soft, rich, oily flesh. Highly nutritious and palatable, it makes them popular with aquatic predators. It also makes them a safe, sustainable seafood choice for humans.

The herring fights population depletion by being a wildly fertile fish. The average female lays between 20,000 and 50,000 eggs each year. The extremely prolific may deposit up to 200,000 eggs, all of which are externally fertilized by the male. The female deposits her eggs on seaweed, rock, gravel, shells and sand. Adhesive in nature, the eggs attach themselves to these substrates. In the North Atlantic lobstermen regularly find the sticky roe clinging to their lobster traps. Unusually heavy for fish eggs, they sink to the ocean bottom, creating a dense mat up to several centimetres in thickness. This carpet may contain millions of eggs from numerous herring.

Herring reach maturity at the age of four or five years. This is when their reproduction ritual begins. Depending upon the species, they may spawn in coastal waters or migrate from the ocean to freshwater rivers to breed. In the latter scenario they are called anadromous, meaning that they move from salt to fresh water to spawn. Salmon, striped bass, sturgeon and shad also follow this routine. In the case of Pacific herring, once a year they head inland to estuaries where they breed. Atlantic herring reproduce in coastal waters and offshore banks.

Typically, herring spawn in waters less than 91 m (300 ft) deep. Plucky travellers, they may swim thousands of kilometres to return to their usual breeding grounds. In some instances these locations have remain unchanged for millennia. Yet in spite of their reputation for predictable spawning routes, herring can be unreliable, switching their breeding locale for no obvious reason. It could be a change in the current, temperature, nutrients or salinity that causes them to abandon a site. Because of the fish's fickleness, regions may experience a glut of herring for several years and then wake one morning to find that the stock has disappeared. Industries dependent upon the herrings' return are devastated when the fish vanish. So, too, are the people who rely upon them for their livelihoods.

Although where herring spawn may be capricious, when they do it is not. Timing depends upon the fish's location or latitude. In the Pacific the season takes place from late January to July, and in the Atlantic from August to November.

The incubation periods are similarly reliant upon locale and temperature. In waters 7°C (45°F) or colder, the fish may incubate for as long as forty days. If the water is warmer, around 10°C (50°F), and if the eggs aren't gobbled up by cod, flounder, haddock, crabs and starfish, the herring will hatch in seven to ten days.

Within the herring community egg mortality is high. Those on top of the heap risk being picked off by the aforementioned predators who see the lush blanketing of eggs as a lavish, protein-packed buffet. Those on the bottom of the stack receive less oxygen. Deprived of this necessity, they may not hatch. If they do, they may be smaller and less developed than the larvae from the topside eggs.

The larvae that do hatch will be about 6 mm, or a quarter of an inch, in size. With the exception of their eyes, the larvae are transparent. Delicate creatures, they spend their first few days attached to a yolk sac. During this period they are negatively buoyant and remain in deep waters.

As their yolk sacs dwindle, their digestive systems develop and they begin to eat plankton. At this stage they are weak swimmers – in truth, they float, rather than swim, in the water

– and are once again at risk. Some researchers believe that only 1 per cent of larvae reach the juvenile stage.

Herring larvae live the first three to eleven months of their life near their spawning and hatching grounds. During this period their scales form and turn an iridescent blue-green colour. The fish begin to establish the schools in which they will travel and live for the majority of their lives. By the age of one year they will have grown to about 10 cm (4 in.) in size. At this point they will set out in groups to explore and feast in the waters beyond their birth site.

Separated from their protective habitat, young herring become fair game for admirers of their soft, fatty flesh. Since medieval times, no fan has been more passionate about herring than man. For millennia humans have adored the delicate flavour of young, small herring and the meatier tang of the older, bigger fish. At Scandinavian excavation sites herring

The fishing village of Klädesholmen, Sweden, 1862.

bones dating back to 3000 BC have been unearthed, providing physical proof that man has had an extensive history with this fish.

The first time herring appeared in print was in AD 240. The third-century Roman historian Solinus had described the people of the Scottish Hebrides as 'living on fish and milk', with that fish being herring. Further written and physical evidence indicates that innumerable generations of Europeans staved off famine by catching and eating this omega-3-rich fish. Records show that by the twelfth century herring had become a staple of European diets, consumed alongside another mainstay, bread. Through preservation efforts and innovations, this fish would become a portable and, subsequently, powerful food.

The medieval populace would have struggled to find something as nourishing as this tiny fish. According to the United States Department of Agriculture, an 85-gram or 3-ounce portion of cooked herring contains 19.6 grams of protein, 9.9 grams of fat and 173 calories. Of the fat, only 2.2 grams is saturated. The remaining is healthy unsaturated fats such as omega-3 fatty acids. Studies show that these poly-unsaturated fats contribute to cardiovascular well-being.

Herring contains high amounts of phosphorus, potassium and selenium. The last mineral aids in the construction of DNA and fights free radicals in our bodies. The fish also has 76 per cent of the daily nutritional value of vitamin D and four times the daily requirement of vitamin B12. Like selenium, vitamin B12 assists in making DNA and maintains blood health. While our forebears may not have realized it, they were eating an extremely wholesome food.

Sustenance wasn't herring's only function. It acted as barter, payment, ransom and reward. During the Middle Ages, from the fifth to the fifteenth century, its economic

Amsterdam in 1890.

importance rivalled that of spices. Its impact extended into the Renaissance period as well. In 'The Herring and Its Effect on the History of Britain, 1918', A. M. Samuel claimed that 'Wool and herring in the period covered by the twelfth to seventeenth century were what would now be called key industries.'

Because of herring, settlements and societies sprang up along thousands of miles of coastline. Assemble enough fishermen and their families in one spot and they form camps, then communities, then villages and so on. Amsterdam, Copenhagen, Belgium's Ostend, Lowestoft and Great Yarmouth in England and Molde in Norway are just a few of the towns and cities that owe their existence to herring.

In the thirteenth century the Danish writer Saxo Grammaticus described how shoals in the Danish Sound or Øresund, the stretch of water separating Copenhagen from Malmö, Sweden, were so dense that ships struggled to navigate their way through them. In describing these monumental schools of fish, Flemish sailors would say, 'It is as if the dunes set sail.' Men landed herring here by the thousands of tons.

Even though the herring supply seemed endless, medieval fishermen clung to superstitions and rituals to ensure a healthy catch. Some believed that the more fleas in a fisherman's clothes, the more fish he would catch. If a fisherman found one or two fleas, he would land only a handful of fish. Another myth involved mentioning salmon or rabbit on the fishing boat: if anyone on board said one of these words, all would return to shore empty-handed.

Often these notions were region-specific. Scottish fishermen en route to their boats would avoid anyone dressed in black. Black meant few, if any, herring would be found. In England, if a fisherman had a dismal day at sea, he went home and made, hanged and burned effigies of those whom he believed had ruined the fishing venture. Besides observing

Ostend, Belgium, in 1890.

Modern fish weir.

these rites, early fishermen took another step to ensure a good catch. Since the herring were too small to be obtained by a hook and line or spear, the men set up traps or nets. For centuries Native Americans placed traps known as weirs along North America's northeast shoreline. Made from sticks stuck into the soft, wet ground with plants and branches woven through them, the weir traps were erected when the tide went out. At high tide the traps captured droves of fish that were collected when the tide receded.

Vikings and Saxons also utilized weir traps. Texts and illustrations from the early Middle Ages show that the Vikings made slight modifications to this system. Their weirs channelled fish through one large chamber and into another. The second chamber emptied the fish into a basket-like wicker trap.

Further evidence of trapping exists half a mile off England's South Essex coast. Erected by Anglo-Saxons between the seventh and the tenth century, the complex series of fish traps consists of roughly 13,000 timber posts. Such a large system would have brought in several hundred thousand fish each year. Because of this astounding number historians assume that the herring were hauled in for commercial purposes and not intended for feeding the local population alone.

Other early fishing gear consisted of drift and seine nets. A drift net is exactly what it sounds like – a net drifting in the water into which fish swim and become trapped. Hanging vertically, the modern drift net is kept in place by floats on the top of the net, at the water's surface, and by weights attached to the net's bottom to keep the net submerged.

In regions where massive schools existed, a fisherman might haul out a purse seine. Possessing a drawstring, this large net encircled and, by pulling on the string, enclosed the fish. The net was then dragged onto a small, open boat where the fisherman sorted through his catch.

Fishermen now acknowledge the environmental drawbacks of these methods. Although it is a passive, inexpensive

Second World War-era herring boat with seine nets in Barclay Sound, British Columbia.

Herring net on display at the National Museum of Denmark in Copenhagen.

Fishing boat and purse seine from the 1960s.

and highly efficient way to fish, drift netting yields a significant amount of by-catch. This term refers to all untargeted fish and aquatic life that may become tangled up in and perish as a result of fishing nets. By-catch includes any fish larger than the intended catch as well as sea birds, sea lions, seals, sharks, dolphins and whales. Obviously, the smaller the targeted fish is, the smaller the net and the greater the by-catch will be.

As with drift nets, significant by-catch occurs with purse seines. Plus, if left unchecked, the amount of fish trapped in a purse seine could decimate a herring stock. Many countries now regulate the use of purse seines, banning them near shorelines and ecologically sensitive areas.

By the fifteenth century trawlers had begun to usurp hand-tossed nets and timber traps. Trawlers are large boats fitted with nets that they tow through the water. When boats drag their nets along the ocean floor, they are classified as bottom trawlers. Bottom trawlers capture such ocean floor-dwelling or demersal fish as cod, haddock, squid and octopus. If the boats pull their nets through the middle of the ocean's water column, culling pelagic fish such as herring, mackerel,

Modern fishing trawlers in Skagen, Denmark.

shrimp and tuna, they are called mid-water or pelagic trawlers. Both types have been likened to vacuum cleaners in their ability to collect vast quantities of fish.

Akin to other netting techniques, trawling has been criticized for the immense amount of by-catch that it garners. It has also been castigated for the destruction of habitat and damage caused to the ocean floor. Even so, trawling persists throughout the world.

2

Herring's Sway over Medieval Europe

Considered a primitive fish, one that has existed for over 150 million years, herring is believed to have fed mankind in the northern hemisphere since prehistoric times. Even so, it is difficult to pinpoint exactly where man first started fishing for herring. Roughly half a million herring bones dating back 10,000 years have been unearthed in British Columbia, Alaska and Washington state. Bones and fishing tools of a similar age have been found in Denmark, Norway and western Sweden. These skeletons point to the early existence of healthy herring populations, organized fisheries and the use of nets. The common time frames and findings over 7,000 km apart complicate the determination of who first spotted the worthiness of this fish.

Undoubtedly, our ancestors appreciated this tasty and abundant food source. As early as the sixth century European churches offered prayers for fruitful herring catches. This tradition continued into the nineteenth century when, in 1861, Joseph George Cumming wrote of the 3,600 fishermen on the Isle of Man in the Irish Sea receiving a prayer in the weekly litany for 'the blessings of the sea'. The men also had their own special prayer, composed by Anglican bishop Thomas Wilson and recited before they stepped into their boats and headed off. The invocations must have worked, for in the 1880s the men brought in 40,000 barrels of herring. Each barrel contained eight hundred fish.

The English coastal town of Great Yarmouth, known historically as Yarmouth, likewise owes its creation and prosperity to this fish. Starting in the sixth century, fishermen established camps near the broad estuary where the River Yare empties into the North Sea. At this location they docked their boats, laid out their nets and set out to fish for herring. Archaeological evidence indicates that they erected huts for drying, salting, smoking and selling their catches.

The men constructed a modest chapel on the beach at which they gave thanks for their bounty. In the early twelfth century a larger, more elaborate church, St Nicholas's, which was later renamed the Great Yarmouth Minster, was built to serve the seafaring community. As the patron saint of sailors and those whose livelihoods depend upon the sea, St Nicholas was an aptly chosen saint.

Great Yarmouth, Norfolk, in the 19th century, with its bustling market and majestic Great Yarmouth Minster in the background.

Herring contributed not only to the construction of Yarmouth but to its status as a town. In return for an annual fee of ten milliers, or ten thousand, herring, Henry 1 made Yarmouth a burgh or self-governing region in 1108. By the thirteenth century the payment had changed to a hundred herring baked in 24 pies. Yarmouth's town seal depicted a ship traversing herring-filled waters.

Payment in herring became a common practice throughout coastal areas. To gain and maintain the right to fish for herring near a port town, fishermen gave a portion of their catch to the local mayor. In turn, the mayors of these towns paid a tithe in herring to the church. The citizens of Beccles in Suffolk, which in the early Middle Ages maintained a prosperous herring fishery, handed over a yearly rent of 30,000 herring to the Abbey of St Edmond. The amount was subsequently increased to 60,000 herring per year.

Restitution in herring wasn't restricted to England. In eleventh-century France a saltworks outside the seaside city of Dieppe donated five billion salted herring to Rouen's Abbey of St Catherine. As in England, France had vibrant herring settlements. It also had stupendous tales of lone fishermen collecting upwards of 800,000 herring in their nets in one morning.

In medieval times giving fish to the clergy made perfect sense. Back then the Church forbade the consumption of meat on Wednesday, Friday and Saturday. It likewise opposed the eating of meat during Lent and Advent. As a result, Christians, including monks, priests and other clergymen, went without meat in their diets for 195 days a year. Thanks to the tithing of herring, the faithful had a rich source of protein for these days of abstinence.

Because medieval cooks used salted herring in their recipes, their fasting meals frequently left diners feeling parched.

Barrel of
salted herring.

To slake their thirst, people reached for the safest, most abundant drink on offer: ale or wine. As a result, herring unintentionally turned periods of temperance into times of insobriety.

As the centuries passed, herring would become synonymous not with drunkenness but with monotonous meals served during religious fasts. The fault lay not with the fish but with the uninspired cooks preparing it. They routinely doled out round after round of salted herring simmered with chopped onion and slabs of salted or smoked herring dressed with mustard or parsley sauce. Those with access to fresh herring did slightly better, serving grilled or fried herring dressed with one of the ubiquitous sauces as well as fish pie, soup and stew. However, there are far more and delicious ways to work with this fish.

Along with nourishing the devout, herring provided sustenance to the peasants of Europe. Because their farm animals were more valuable alive and busy laying eggs, providing milk and ploughing fields than they were dead and in farmers' stomachs, peasants rarely killed and ate their livestock. For a nutrient- and energy-packed food they looked to herring.

In Scandinavia herring and cod were the main fish of the Viking age. Many historians speculate that the Vikings set sail first and foremost to net cod and herring. Conquering lands was an extension of their quest to acquire fish and gain fishing grounds.

Excavations at the Viking settlement and trading center Hedeby, on the border of Germany and Denmark, show that the majority of seafood consumed there was herring. On Denmark's Roskilde Fjord, where the remains of five Viking ships were unearthed in 1962, archaeologists found evidence of herring consumption dating back to the 700s. Herring bones account for 18 per cent of the artefacts recovered on the fjord from the eighth and ninth centuries. That number increases to 42 per cent in the tenth and eleventh centuries, pointing to the fish's plenitude and rising importance to the Vikings.

During this period herring would have been considered simple, everyday food for the Vikings. They would have eaten the fish freshly caught, salted or smoked. Old Norse poems mention herring being consumed alongside oats, a practice that lived on in seventeenth-century Danish cookbooks.

The Vikings pursued herring not only along the coasts of Denmark, Norway and Sweden, but on England's east coast and Scotland's Orkney Islands. Historians believe that England's mammoth herring shoals drew marauding Vikings to its eastern shores in the eighth century. Sailing in their

Oseberg Viking ship, 9th century, at the Viking Ship Museum in Oslo, Norway.

streamlined, wooden longships, the Vikings came for the fish and to raid the wealthy coastal monasteries, taking their jewels and other riches. The most famous of these attacks occurred in 793 on the holy island of Lindisfarne in the North Sea. The Lindisfarne raid is regularly cited as the beginning of the Viking Age.

Artefacts reveal that Vikings stayed in the regions that they had conquered and created settlements around fishing and farming. On the Orkney island of Westray fish bones from the ninth century suggest that Vikings had caught and salted herring there. They then traded the fish or transported it back to their homelands.

Towards the end of the Viking era, in the twelfth century, southwestern Sweden became home to an annual fish market, the Skåne or Scania Market. Situated on the Falsterbo Peninsula, the market featured herring caught in the adjacent Baltic Sea. Hugely popular in the 1520s, Scania attracted as many as

7,500 fishing boats, averaging five fishermen in each, to Falsterbo.

In an age without refrigeration salting was an easy way to preserve meat and seafood. This was especially true for herring, which, because of its oily composition, was highly perishable and had to be salted as soon as it made it to shore. Although early efforts could be quite crude – some fishermen just dumped the fish and salt together in heaps on the beach in a procedure dubbed 'rousing' or rough salting – they stopped the fish from spoiling. Salting and other types of preservation will be explored in depth later.

At the Scania Market women worked alongside men, preparing the fish for sale. The women would salt and pack the herring into barrels, each of which weighed roughly 60 kg (130 lb). In 1494 they processed an average of 6,500 herring per day for two months.

From August to October the Scandinavian fishermen set up booths and traded or sold their barrels of salted herring

Men salting herring in Ålesund, Norway, c. 1920.

to foreign merchants. The success of the Scania Market turned this region into a major trade hub, a status that would last for 250 years. Because the Falsterbo Peninsula was under Danish rule, the market made the kingdom of Denmark exceedingly wealthy. By the twelfth century its herring-based affluence had inspired countries such as England, France and the Netherlands to attempt to get rich with 'the silver of the sea'.

The Scania Market fostered a medieval trade association known as the Hanseatic League. Formed in 1241 by the German merchants of Hamburg on the North Sea and of Lübeck on the Baltic, the League aimed to safeguard the businessmen's mutual commercial interests. One of these pursuits was the catching and selling of herring. Through the use of its member cities' armies, the League protected fishing and trade routes from thieves and pirates. It also enabled merchants to set up offices and warehouses in sister ports. This permitted business transactions to take place without interrupted communication, misunderstandings and other impediments to commerce.

The Hanseatic League represented roughly two hundred cities in Northwestern Europe. In its heyday its reach extended as far west as Bruges, now in Belgium, and as far eastward as Novgorod in Russia. It included offices in London and Bergen, Norway. Headquartered in Lübeck, which featured three herring on a gold shield as its town seal, it was governed by the Hansetag, the council that dealt with trade issues.

While its objectives of secure trade routes and shared commercial ventures might sound benign, the Hanseatic League monopolized the sale and transport of herring. It did this for two centuries, delivering barrels of salted herring to cities as far and as influential as Rome. As was previously mentioned, this fish was indispensable to Christians during their fast days. Devout Christians and Catholics were equally critical to the success of the herring market and the Hanseatic League.

Although herring played a crucial role in the League's success, the association did deal in other products, including furs, cloth, salt, wax, honey and metal ore. Overall, though, its triumphs and failures correlated to the boom and bust of herring. When the fifteenth-century herring population plummeted in the Baltic Sea, the power of the League declined. By the seventeenth century it had lost the bulk of its members. Only three German cities, Lübeck, Bremen and Hamburg, remained in the League until the very end. By 1862 it had ceased to exist.

In spite of the dwindling influence of the Hanseatic League, Europeans continued to crave, and obtain, herring. When the supply of Baltic Sea fish evaporated, countries sought other fishing grounds. In 1540 Dutch fishermen scored a major win when they encountered herring shoals off the English coast in the North Sea. Their discovery spurred the Netherlands to construct more and better fishing boats and to direct additional fishermen to this region. By the end of the sixteenth century the Netherlands would be one of the richest, most powerful nations in Europe, due, in large part, to herring. Over 1,600 of its ships would deliver herring to countries such as France, England, Poland and Russia and return with salt, wool, flax, grain, wine and timber.

Herring also held sway over the country's capital, Amsterdam. Located at the mouth of the Amstel River, Amsterdam got its start as a fishing village in the twelfth century. Because of its handy location on the sea and on inland waterways and major rivers, Amsterdam would assume a major role in catching and exporting herring. The profusion of herring fishing, curing and trading along the banks of the Amstel River led

Amsterdam fish market and bourse or weighing house, *c.* 1890.

to the Dutch claim that their capital was literally built upon the bones of fish.

The Dutch gobbled up herring. A preferred method of preparation, which required no cooking at all, was *maatjes*. This seasonal delicacy consisted of fresh, young, fat herring that had yet to spawn. Custom dictated that *maatjes* be eaten raw as soon as they arrived in port. People would hold them by their tails and, dangling the fish overhead, down them in one or two gulps.

It's been said that the Dutch consume more raw, fresh herring than any other seafood. Even today you'll encounter *haringkar* or herring carts in the Netherlands that specialize in uncooked herring. Unlike in medieval times, the fish has been frozen first to kill off parasites such as flatworms and nematodes.

During the heyday of the Dutch fisheries piscators formed guilds and swore solemn oaths not to fish for foreign countries. They also prohibited foreign workers or spectators on their boats. They alone cleaned and preserved the fish.

In keeping with this level of professionalism the Dutch government established the College of the Fishery to regulate the herring industry in the late sixteenth century. It licensed ships, set quotas and imposed quality controls so that Dutch herring would maintain its reputation for excellence. The College of the Fishery established the departure date of herring fleets at the start of the summer solstice. Amid boisterous singing, prayers, toasts and homes decorated with banners and bunting, Dutch fishermen set sail on 24 June or St John's Day. When they returned with their ships weighed down by hundreds of barrels of fish, a sea of undulating flags welcomed them. The flags had been hoisted onto homes, businesses and government buildings as a homage to the men and their bounty.

Boys eating herring on Weesperplein in Amsterdam, the Netherlands.

Modern-day herring and hot dog cart in Amsterdam.

The tributes didn't end there. Until the twentieth century Dutch fishmongers hung wreaths of box leaves and flags depicting the royal crown over the entrances of their Amsterdam shops. These decorations let everyone know that new herring had arrived. Citizens paid up to a gold ducat apiece for the freshest, youngest and tenderest herring. As the nineteenth-century French historian Jules Michelet stated, 'The herring fishers transmuted their stinking cargoes into gold.'

By the end of the sixteenth century herring had transformed the Netherlands into an economic heavyweight and formidable sea power. The Dutch had come to realize that their large fishing fleet could serve as the foundation for a merchant marine. In peacetime the fleet would engage in its usual fishing pursuits. In times of crisis it would switch to a naval reserve and transport soldiers and war supplies. Eventually, a structured naval school would be established to train men to protect the Netherlands.

The eighteenth-century French naturalist Bernard-Germain-Étienne de La Ville sur-Ilan, Comte de Lacépède, succinctly summed up herring's importance to the Dutch and all of Europe:

The herring is one of those products whose use decides the destiny of empires. The coffee bean, the tea leaf, the spices of the torrid zones, the worm which spins silks, had less influence on the wealth of nations than the northern ocean.

3
The Herring Cure

With so many herring being caught, sold and shipped, the question of food preservation invariably needed to be addressed. All fish begin to deteriorate when they leave the water. Their tissues break down and bacteria develop. To avert decomposition and spoilage, fishermen promptly and thoroughly clean the fish after catching them. Once the fish have been gutted, all the moisture must be removed. This will thwart bacterial growth: bacteria need a damp environment to survive and prosper.

In ancient and medieval times fish were air-dried for days, if not weeks, until all the water had evaporated and no bacteria could possibly exist. Unfortunately, herring does not respond well to drying. Due to its high fat content, if placed outdoors to dry, the gutted herring quickly becomes rancid. This trait sets it apart from another important medieval fish, cod. After being cleaned, cod could be splayed out on wooden racks and left outside to dry until hardened. When dried, cod was known as stockfish. The name resulted either from the wood on which the cod was dried or because, when dry, it was as hard as a stick. In Old English *stock* meant a log, stump or post, while in Old Norse it referred to a tree trunk. Dried cod had a 'shelf life' of several years.

Since herring had no chance at becoming stockfish, another ancient form of dehydration had to be used. This was salting. Salt draws out the moisture from herring through osmosis. If you add enough salt to the fish, the flesh dries out and bacteria stop breeding in it. Salt also deters the introduction of any new microbes.

To kill off bacteria and prohibit its growth, you typically need a salt concentration of 20 per cent. If you catch and clean 100 kg of herring, you will need 20 kg of salt to cure it. With medieval fishermen bringing in fish by the hundreds of thousands, salt became vital to the success of herring.

A simple way to obtain salt was to evaporate seawater. Since ancient times salt has been extracted in this manner. Ancient Romans boiled seawater in ceramic pots called *briquetage* until solid blocks of salt formed. They then smashed the pottery and pulled out the salt. The Romans also constructed shallow salt ponds along the Mediterranean Sea. There the

Men salting herring, mid-20th century.

sun and wind would evaporate the water, leaving behind layers of salt. The Romans raked up these salt crystals and stored them for later use. The Romans' evaporation methods continued through the Middle Ages, with medieval Europeans employing many of the same ponds that their predecessors had built.

In colder, drearier lands people could not rely upon nature to vaporize seawater and furnish them with salt. Instead they cooked down large quantities of water to extract the coveted mineral. The English put their salt water in shallow lead pans and brought it to a boil over open fires. When the liquid evaporated, it left behind salt. Depending on the temperature of the water and rate of evaporation, the open pan process, as it was called, could produce both fine and coarse salt. The latter was used for curing fish.

The English also engaged in a laborious practice known as sleeching. With sleeching, sand from the coastlines was collected, air-dried and then placed in a pit, or kinch, lined with straw. Seawater was poured over the sand until a briny mixture flowed out. This brine was collected and boiled in pans over wood- or peat-fuelled fires until all that remained was salt.

The people of England weren't the only northern Europeans to boil water for salt. Wherever there was a spring or pond, people boiled down water to evaporate it and collected the leftover salt.

During the Middle Ages Germany and Sweden began a two-way trading system based upon salt. The Germans had salt and lots of it. Meanwhile, the Scandinavians had herring. German merchants took this mineral from the country's Lübeck salt springs, sold it to Scania fishermen and bought the resulting salted herring from them. Their partnership was seamless in its simplicity.

Salting fish to preserve it for future use.

Salt preserved the herring, allowing it to be stored during temperate months and consumed in Northern Europe's frigid winter season. It also enabled the fish to be transported to regions beyond the coastlines. Due to its portability and affordability, salted herring became part of countless inland diets.

As you might expect from a food desiccated by sodium chloride, herring could take on a hard, tough texture. Before being cooked and consumed, the fish was reconstituted by soaking in hot water overnight or by being boiled. In both cases the water had to be changed several times. Even then the fish might retain an overly salty taste or chewy consistency.

In the fourteenth century Dutch fisherman Willem Beukelszoon introduced a revolutionary technique for cleaning and preserving herring. Known as *haringkaken*, herring gutting, or colloquially as zipping, he gutted freshly caught herring so that the throat, gills and long gut were removed. Beukelszoon then brined the fish – meaning that he placed the fish in heavily salted water and allowed it to steep – in wooden barrels to preserve it. Processing the herring on the spot avoided lengthy and costly journeys to shore when the fishing season was short and the loss of time resulted in a considerable loss of profit. Beukelszoon's method meant that the price of an inexpensive food could be reduced even more. Along with saving time and money, brining didn't dry out the herring as salting did. It also didn't require hours of steeping or boiling in clean water to remove the salt. Furthermore, it kept the fish safe for consumption.

History credits Beukelszoon with creating zipping and brining. It also heralds him as a game-changer in the world of herring. Even so, almost every country that has ever fished for herring, including France, Norway and Iceland, has claimed this as its own invention. Documents from eleventh- and twelfth-century France and England speak of fishermen cleaning their fish and placing them in a salty seawater solution to preserve them. Regardless, Beukelszoon is still considered the originator of herring brines.

Beukelszoon's influence ranges beyond curing, storing and transporting fish. He may have facilitated the creation of several herring specialities, including Swedish *surströmming* or soured herring. In existence since at least the sixteenth century, *surströmming* is composed of gutted and decapitated Baltic herring that have been submerged in a strong brine for less than 24 hours. After the desired time has passed, the fish are removed from the brine and placed in a weaker marinade for approximately one month. In midsummer the herring are deposited into airtight barrels or, as is more common today, cans. Deprived of air, the fish begins to ferment. This fermentation is the final step in preserving the fish.

If you happen upon *surströmming* in a Swedish market, you won't forget it. The gases that build up in these cans

Because of its tremendous stench, *surströmming* is often opened outdoors.

cause the tops to bulge and the tins to take on the shape of a ball. If you have ever stood near someone opening a can of *surströmming*, you will always remember that experience, too. You may, though, wish to forget it. Fermented herring gives off an acrid odour reminiscent of rotten eggs or decaying meat, and it has a heavy, cheesy taste. Its pungency has caused the fish to be banned in some public spaces. Airlines have forbidden it on planes, stating that the pressurized can of *surströmming* could explode at high altitudes and injure passengers. It could also produce a big stink.

German food writer Wolfgang Fassbender has said that the hardest aspect of *surströmming* is overcoming the urge to vomit from the horrendous stench before getting to discover what the herring actually tastes like. Not much of an endorsement, is it? In any case, fermented herring remains part of Sweden's culinary scene.

To properly enjoy *surströmming*, open the can outdoors so that the smell doesn't linger in your kitchen. Once the can has been opened, drain off the liquid. Rinse the fish under cold, running water and pat the fillets dry with a clean cloth. Place the fish on a plate and scatter chopped red onion over each fillet (onion somewhat masks the odour and tempers the flavour). Custom dictates that you should serve *surströmming* with small, cooked potatoes, thin, crisp bread known as *tunnbröd* and butter.

If eating *surströmming* straight from the can sounds unappealing, you can add it to the classic *smørrebrød*. Accompanied by boiled potatoes, diced onions, strong cheese and a glass of lager, aquavit or vodka, a fermented herring open-face sandwich makes a memorable meal.

While *surströmming* and Swedes may owe a nod of thanks to Willem Beukelszoon and his herring brines, other countries have outright honoured the man. Roughly two centuries after Beukelszoon's invention, Charles v, ruler of the Holy Roman Empire, visited the Dutch fisherman's grave. There he decreed that a monument should be erected in his memory. Today, if you visit Beukelszoon's home town of Biervliet in the Netherlands, you may spot a bronze statue of a seated fisherman dressed in a raincoat, rain hat, apron and boots, holding a fish in one hand and a knife in the other. Resting on a stone base in the town market, this is the monument to Willem Beukelszoon.

Brining and salting weren't the only methods of preservation. Fishermen also smoked herring. With this approach the men still had to salt or brine the fish. They then hung the herring up in their smokehouses and left them there to dry and take on a smoky tang. With smoking the amount of time spent in salt or a salty mixture was reduced. Plus smoking added complexity to the texture and taste and offered a change from the usual salty herring.

In Sweden smoked Baltic herring is called *böckling* and is made into a savoury smoked herring-and-egg pudding named, sensibly enough, *böckling* pudding. While this type of smoked herring may not sound familiar, in all likelihood red herring will. In existence long before the eponymous idiom, the moniker red herring comes from the colour of the smoked fish's flesh. Red herring is herring that has been smoked for such a long time that it has turned crimson.

Several countries contend that they invented red herring. The English allege that an anonymous thirteenth-century fisherman from Yarmouth created the first red herring by accident. He had hung up his spare catch in the rafters of his hot smokehouse. Forgetting about the fish, he had left them in the warm, smoky chamber for several days. During that time they turned from soft, silvery, highly perishable fish to dry, red, fish-shaped planks that were impervious to temperature, time and bugs of any kind. As this nameless fisherman learned at first hand, the longer you smoke herring, the redder and harder it gets.

It is a charming anecdote, one that in all likelihood bears some truth. Nonetheless, the English may not have been the first to stumble upon this treatment. At least a century earlier the French were making *hareng saur*, smoked herring.

Whole smoked herring on display at London's Borough Market.

The streets of twelfth-century Paris resounded with cries of 'Herring, smoked or newly salted.' The French dubbed their smoked herring, among other names, *gendarmes*. The reason for this particular label is uncertain. It may have to do with the red in the officer's uniform or the stiff, upright position held by both man and smoked fish. Coincidentally, folks in Yarmouth nicknamed red herring 'militiamen' while the Scots referred to them as 'Glasgow magistrates'.

Whether from France, England or elsewhere, the process for making red herring remained the same. The fish was salted, suspended from rods over slow fires and smoked. After the initial smoking the herring rested for two days before being smoked again. This routine continued until the fish achieved the preferred dark red colour and dry consistency. The resulting dehydrated fish could endure humidity and warm temperatures without becoming rancid. It could also tolerate the rough modes of medieval transport.

The arrival of refrigeration in the nineteenth century would end the necessity of such a harsh cure. Even so, red herring is still produced and shipped to regions where refrigeration isn't a given and temperatures soar. It maintains a fairly strong presence in African and Caribbean cooking, whose cuisines it is believed to have entered via trade.

Before being consumed, red herring requires a small amount of prep work. Using a sharp knife, slice off the head and tail. Next, pull off the skin. If you prefer delicate tasting fish, you should soak the herring before filleting it. Old cookbooks recommend leaving it in hot beer for a minimum of two hours and a maximum of two days. A few suggest steeping the fish in buttermilk or cold tea.

A recipe from the 1963 version of *Mrs Beeton's Everyday Cookery* offers another classic approach. To start, cover the red herring with boiling water. After several minutes drain off the water and pour warm milk over the herring. Leave the fish to soak for one hour. Once the hour has passed, skin and fillet the herring and cut it into pieces. Dress the fish with oil and vinegar and garnish it with chopped egg yolks and chopped gherkins. If you don't like egg or gherkins, you can toss the herring with diced boiled potatoes.

As for how red herring slipped into the English vernacular and came to mean a diversion or smokescreen, several hypotheses exist. One has an escaped prisoner tricking pursuant hounds by covering his tracks with the scent of red herring. The smell diverted the dogs onto the wrong path and allowed the convict to sneak away. Another explanation has medieval hunters training dogs to track their quarry by making false and real trails with red herring. In *The Sportsman's Dictionary: Or The Gentleman's Companion* from 1686 Nicholas Cox describes this training practice as 'The trailing or dragging of a dead Cat, or Fox, (and in case of necessity a Red-Herring) three or four miles . . . and then laying the Dogs on the scent.'

A third theory involves a seventeenth-century English clergyman and a dirty trick played on his servant. In his will the archdeacon of Chichester, Jasper Mayne, bequeathed a trunk to his long-time attendant. The container was said to contain 'something that would make him drink'. When the man lifted the trunk's lid, he found a single smoked herring inside. His inheritance was literally a red herring.

While mystery surrounds red herring, the English kipper has a very straightforward history. In 1843 John Woodger of Newcastle upon Tyne took a salmon-curing process and adapted it for herring, thus creating the kippered herring or kipper. The mildest of all smoked herring, kippers were split down their backs, as opposed to their bellies, and gutted. After being cleaned, they were submerged in brine for a minimum of 30 minutes. The brining time was determined by the

Advertisement for Scottish kippered herring, late 19th century.

fattiness of the fish. Fatter herring required longer brining to ensure that they didn't spoil.

Removed from the solution, the fish were hung on hooks and smoked over slow oak fires for an average of twelve hours. When finished, the herring acquired the copper hue for which they were named. In Middle English a reddish-brown colour was referred to as *kypre*.

Woodger's approach resulted in a smoked fish that retained the shelf life, but not the hard, slab-like consistency, of red herring. His fish didn't require hours upon hours of soaking to reconstitute. Lighter in flavour and texture, they were perfect for anyone preferring milder foods.

With this approach Woodger set up a lucrative kippering business, John Woodger and Sons Ltd, in Northeast England. Each year he would ship over 20 million kippers to London and its neighbouring communities. The kipper has long been considered the king of the English breakfast. Grilled, baked or boiled and served on buttered toast, it continues to provide a cheap yet savoury and nutritious start to the day.

Kippers also play a part in English teas. Although cooks tend to present them alongside a pot of hot tea, they are said to go equally well with a glass of whisky. Some swear by using alcohol as a sauce and pour gin over their fish.

Less than a hundred years into the history of kippers, manufacturers began conjuring up ways to cut costs for this already inexpensive seafood. During the last days of the First World War kipperers, or kipper makers, began to dye the fish their unmistakable copper colour. To do this, they dipped the herring into the vegetable annatto. Culled from the seed casings of the Brazilian achiote tree, annatto imparts an orange-red colour to anything with which it comes in contact.

The benefit of dyeing versus smoking herring was twofold. When properly smoked, herring lost 15 to 20 per cent of its weight – all of which was water weight – in the smoke-house. If dye was applied to the herring, the fish maintained its weight. The herring didn't need to stay in the kiln very long

A breakfast of kippers and potato cakes in York, England.

to achieve its coppery colour; that had already been attained with the dye. Shorter time spent in the smokehouse meant that the herring retained more moisture and weight. As a result, fewer kippers were needed to fill a box. Kipperers could charge the same amount for less fish.

Dyeing stretched the kipper supply for the manufacturers but short-changed the customers. People expected to buy and receive smoked, rather than dyed, fish. In addition to being duped about how the kippers achieved their copper colour, they got fewer kippers for the same price. If these deceptions weren't bad enough, the consumers wound up with kippers that were bogged down by excess moisture and didn't keep.

Sadly, in order to compete with the unscrupulous producers churning out cheap, coloured kippers, all others had to follow suit. By 1930 very few true, undyed kippers remained. What consumers purchased were 'painted ladies', the name given to these adulterated fish.

What brought back authentic kippers was a 1955 article in the *Sunday Times* on smoked salmon. After the piece ran, a reader from the coastal town of Lowestoft sent a box of freshly smoked, undyed kippers to the *Sunday Times*. The following week *The Times* published another smoked fish story, this time on the loveliness of legitimately smoked Lowestoft kippers. Public interest was piqued. As a result, the Lowestoft kipperer became inundated with orders and, with that, true kippers had returned.

Kippers are reputed to have the longevity of red herring and the palatability of a bloater. The latter's unflattering name stems from its plump, almost bloated appearance as well as from the Swedish word *blöta*, which means 'to soak'. The French ports north of Normandy specialize in a similar herring product called *bouffi*, which also stands for 'swollen' or 'bloated'. Originally, bloaters were referred to as bloat fish.

In the past, where you resided determined how you prepared your bloaters. In Wales people covered their herring with a thick layer of salt. In Great Yarmouth they placed the fish in brine that contained just enough salt to enable the fish to float. In both scenarios wood was placed on top of the fish to weigh it down. The fish was then left to macerate for a day. After 24 hours the herring was washed, dried and briefly cold smoked at temperatures ranging from 20 to 30°C (68 to 86°F). The resulting fish bore faintly smoky and gamey flavours. The funky taste was caused by the presence of stomach and intestinal enzymes in the fish. Unlike red herring and kippers, bloaters were not gutted before being smoked. In addition to their unique taste, bloaters differed in colour from other smoked fish, possessing a straw-like hue. They also had a shorter shelf life. When refrigerated, they lasted for about ten days.

The custom with bloaters was to hang them in front of an open fire with a plate of toast beneath them. When ready, the fish would drip onto the toast, which, in turn, flavoured it. A more modern approach is to split the fish, slide them under a grill and baste them with butter until hot.

Another cure for herring is buckling. A German creation, buckling consists of ungutted but beheaded herring brined for 30 minutes and hot smoked at a temperature ranging from 52 to 80°C (126 to 176°F), for four hours. Hot smoking partially cooks the fish and causes the skin to buckle. A final blast of dense smoke turns the herring golden in colour. Because the fish has not been gutted, it, like a bloater, has a musty taste and a shorter storage life.

Like the bloater, kipper and red herring, the buckling is a breakfast speciality. Germans pair bucklings, or *Bucklinge*, with dark rye bread and butter. They also partner them with scrambled eggs and fried potatoes. Served cold, they go well with horseradish, tomato and cucumber or a tossed salad.

Of all the preservation methods, the one that I encounter most involves pickling. Pickled herring begins as smoked herring does, with salted fish. In this case fillets, rather than the whole herring, are used. The salted fillets are soaked in cold water for six to twelve hours before being placed in a mixture of vinegar, sugar and spices. Refrigerated, they marinate for at least 24 hours.

As you might expect from such a straightforward recipe, pickled herring can be made at home. All that's required are salted herring fillets, a marinade, a shallow dish, a refrigerator and a lidded, airtight container. Once pickled and placed in a jar, the herring will keep for months in the refrigerator. As the fish mellows in the marinade, any remaining small bones will soften, if not dissolve, in the acidic solution. Velvety in texture and delicately sweet, pickled herring melts on your tongue.

No one person has ever stepped forward and claimed that, after years of putting vegetables into jars with vinegar and seasonings, he decided to branch out and try doing the

Assortment of pickled herring in Oslo, Norway.

Danish pickled herring platter.

same with herring. Records indicate, though, that pickled herring first got its start in medieval Europe. Like brining, pickling enabled the herring to be packed into barrels, transported lengthy distances and stored for considerable amounts of time.

A myriad of cuisines feature pickled herring. Dutch, German, Scottish, Russian, Polish and Nordic cooking are among those that add it to appetizers, salads and sandwiches or serve it as a snack. In Jewish cuisine it stars in chopped herring, a spread of puréed pickled herring, eggs, apples, onions and breadcrumbs, and in *schmaltz*. Like *maatjes*, *schmaltz* is made of young herring caught right before spawning and contains at least 18 per cent fat. Unlike the Dutch delicacy, the herring in *schmaltz* is filleted, salted and pickled before being consumed.

Of all the countries infatuated with pickled herring, Denmark is especially famous. You'll come across pickled

Herring *smørrebrød*.

herring in Danish markets, at pavement food stalls, in upscale restaurants and on *kolde bords*, the equivalent of the Swedish smorgasbord. A common statement among Danes is that there are more Danish herring marinades than there are days of the year.

In Denmark dinners frequently begin with a herring course. No *smørrebrød* platter would be complete without pickled herring. Rye bread acts as the base of these open-face sandwiches. While some Danes swear by lard, others employ the less-controversial butter as their *smørrebrød* spread. It's said that a shot of aquavit should be drunk alongside pickled herring and that it aids in digestion, washing the herring down into the stomach.

As well as purchasing or making pickled herring fillets, you can buy rollmops. A German creation, rollmops or *Rollmöpse* start with herring fillets steeped in a vinegar mixture. Removed from the solution, the fillets are rolled up, secured with a toothpick and placed in a fresh marinade containing sliced onions and capers. Rollmops may include cucumber, dill pickles or onion. In the Netherlands they are dressed with a thin layer of mayonnaise, layered on rye bread and paired with a cold beer.

Germany is also home to the Bismarck herring. The story behind this speciality is that Karoline Wiechmann, the wife of a nineteenth-century German trader and brewer, pickled and barrelled fresh Baltic herring fillets behind her husband's bar in Straslund. When her husband Johann won a local lottery, he closed the bar and, inspired by Karoline's pickled herring, opened a fish cannery.

Wiechmann sent a barrel of pickled Baltic herring fillets to Chancellor Otto von Bismarck on his birthday. He later sent another barrel and a letter to Bismarck, asking if he could name his type of pickled herring after the German statesman. Bismarck agreed and Bismarck herring was born.

Bismarck and rollmops are merely two among hundreds, if not thousands, of pickled herring recipes. In Scandinavia pickled herring brings together such diverse ingredients as sour cream, chives, capers, onions, mustard, dill, wine, sherry, tomatoes, orange zest and beetroot. Danish *karrysild*, or curried herring, combines pickled herring with curry paste, mayonnaise, sour cream, sliced apple and spices such as crushed coriander and mustard seeds.

Elsewhere pickled herring accompanies a range of ingredients. The Finnish pâté *vorschmack* mixes pickled herring with minced beef and lamb, garlic, onion, tomato and anchovies. The Russian salad *shuba* or 'herring under a fur coat' has layers of chopped pickled herring, onion, potato and carrot blanketed by beetroot.

In modern Nordic cuisine pickled herring appears in even more intriguing dishes. At the Icelandic restaurant Dill in Reykjavík herring is made into an ice cream that's served alongside pickled herring fillets, pickled shallots and rye-bread crumble. At Copenhagen's acclaimed Noma restaurant pickled herring is wrapped in thin slices of pumpkin and soused with walnut juice. It calls to mind involtini but without all the messy sauces and gloppy cheese. What these and other unique creations show is how versatile this little fish is.

4
Herring Wins and Losses

Unquestionably, herring have influenced the lives of countless men and women. From the fishermen who caught these silver darlings to the peasants who subsisted on them during harsh winters, all saw their futures shaped through this fish. Although history tends to remember the men who worked with herring, a sizeable number of women laboured in the industry, too. The work that they did was every bit as essential to the widespread popularity of the fish.

The most legendary group of women hailed from the British Isles, particularly from Scotland. Known as herring lassies, kipper lassies or Scotch lassies, these women gutted and packed fish. By the mid-nineteenth century the lassies had more or less taken over the processing of herring. This gave the fishermen more time on their boats, which everyone hoped would result in more fish being caught.

Fishermen tracked the herring as they headed down the Scottish coast from the Shetland Islands to Great Yarmouth and from the Outer Hebrides to East Anglia. Wherever the fishermen went, the herring lassies followed. In 1913 over 6,000 women travelled from Scotland and the east coast of Ireland to clean herring. They journeyed by train, moving from port to port for months at a time.

London fishmonger with herring, late 19th century.

Labouring in teams of three, two women gutted the herring while the third placed the fish in wooden barrels and covered them with a layer of salt. Each barrel held between 700 and 1,000 herring. Working ten- to fifteen-hour days in all weather conditions, these efficient and fast-moving workers could fill between 35 and 75 barrels in one day. In 1913 alone lassies in Britain processed over 854 million fish in fourteen weeks. Even for lassies gutting sixteen fish in a minute, this was no small feat.

The female workers were paid nominally and by the hour but given bonuses for the number of barrels packed. During fishing season they worked six days a week with Sundays off. When the herring season ended, their work continued. Although they headed home in late autumn, they spent the winter months mending nets and preparing for the next fishing excursion.

Hardworking, independent and nomadic, the herring lassies were trailblazers for their time. Still, one can't help but wonder why so many women – some as young as thirteen and others over the age of sixty – gravitated to this hardscrabble lifestyle. Working conditions were far from ideal. The salt invariably dried out the skin on the women's hands, causing sores that would blister and chafe. It irritated any cuts that they had sustained from gutting fish. If you've ever unwittingly rubbed salt into a wound, you can attest to how painful a small quantity of good old sodium chloride can be. Having no respite from the salty environment, the women wrapped

Edgar G. Lee, *Sorting Herring, North Shields*, c. 1898.

North Shields fishwives, *c.* 1900.

their hands in strips of linen in an attempt to protect them. These dressings were called 'cloots', which in the Scots language meant rags, cloths or bandages. Even with these bandages, the lassies developed infected lesions.

Salt wasn't the only nuisance. As you might expect from a job that entailed gutting fish, the workers endured copious amounts of blood, scales and stinky fish entrails that sprayed everywhere. In areas such as Yarmouth, where the women stood all day on packed earth that wouldn't drain, decaying detritus pooled at their feet. To cope with all these bodily fluids, the lassies wore aprons, boots and headscarves. These outfits afforded some protection but also left them sweltering on hot, sunny days.

Day in and day out the lassies had to tolerate the stench of dead fish. This putrid odour permeated their clothes, skin and hair. While they grew accustomed to the pungent smell, those outside the fisheries did not. Before the lassies arrived in town with their bags in tow, innkeepers and landlords would take up their good wool carpets and put down cheap straw mats. These would be thrown out after the women, who reeked of dead fish, departed. In general the women were kept apart from other travellers.

Housing was another issue. Often the women ended up in unfurnished, unheated buildings. Some of these stored the herring barrels that they would fill. Bedding, cooking utensils, chairs and the like had to be supplied by the lassies.

In the early twentieth century their lodging situation improved and they began to stay in boarding houses. There they received hot meals and furnished rooms. They still had to pay for their lodging and might share a bed with two other women. Plus they had to buy the food that the cook prepared for them. Notwithstanding, this was a step up from the austere sheds.

In spite of these drawbacks the women took pride in their work and formed strong bonds. Historians have noted how the women would sing together as they processed fish. At night they would gather to knit, dance and sing the songs of their fishing communities. Camaraderie was high and the pay, although not plentiful, was consistent. Through their work the women became independent and beholden to no one but herring. Some women met their spouses through their work and started families. Their offspring frequently went on to fish for or gut herring. In a few instances as many as six generations of one family worked in the herring fisheries.

Overall, herring had a positive impact on the lives of the lassies. There are those, though, whose outcomes weren't as agreeable. These are the men of the herring wars, those who fought and sometimes died for fish.

Prior to 1652, skirmishes had periodically broken out between English and Dutch fishermen racing to land the first herring catch of the season. These fights paled in comparison to the all-out battles that were waged between the two countries over trade routes and fishing rights. Begun in 1652, this series of violent sea conflicts was known as the Anglo-Dutch Wars.

After killing the Dutch Lieutenant-Admiral Maarten Tromp at the Battle of Scheveningen in 1653 and capturing or sinking close to 1,500 Dutch merchant ships, England claimed victory in the first Anglo-Dutch War. With that triumph it gained control of fishing rights in the North Sea. Within just a few years England was catching and processing the bulk of Europe's herring.

In 1665 the Dutch raided St John's, Newfoundland, and put a stop to the herring fishery that England had established there. Eight years later the Dutch invaded another English territory, this time in Ferryland, Newfoundland. The attackers set fire to over thirty fishing boats and loaded their ships with as much fish as they could carry.

The Anglo-Dutch Wars dragged on until 1784. By then the Dutch navy had nearly been decimated. Only twenty ships were left in service. Through the loss of territories, trade routes and fishing rights, the Dutch economy had faltered. Meanwhile, Great Britain had expanded its trading base, acquired a foothold in the East Indies and bolstered its economy.

In the late nineteenth century herring again served as the spoils of war. This time the fight was between Great Britain and the United States over rights to the Atlantic fisheries. As decreed by the Treaty of Washington in 1871, the United States paid the UK $5.5 million for the right to fish the waters of the Gulf of St Lawrence and Newfoundland.

Canned herring from Marshall & Co. in Aberdeen, Scotland.

Unfortunately, not all parties were thrilled by the agreement. Newfoundland fishermen felt that their rights and property had been wrested from them. Without herring they could not earn an income or support their families and would face starvation. Disgruntled and fearful, the Canadians saw no choice but to stage the Fortune Bay Riot.

On 6 January 1878 herring migrated into Newfoundland's Fortune Bay. American fishing schooners, which could lawfully fish in this bay, set out seine nets that were 730 m (2,400 ft) in length and 4.6 m (150 ft) deep. As the Americans had hoped, the large seines quickly filled with fish, ensnaring enough to fill 2,000 barrels. Watching this spectacle from the shoreline were more than two hundred Newfoundland fishermen. Incensed by the Americans' massive catch, which, in turn, was the Canadians' massive loss, the fishermen took to their boats and headed out to confront their nemeses. First they demanded that the Americans release the herring. When this didn't transpire, they commandeered the seines from two

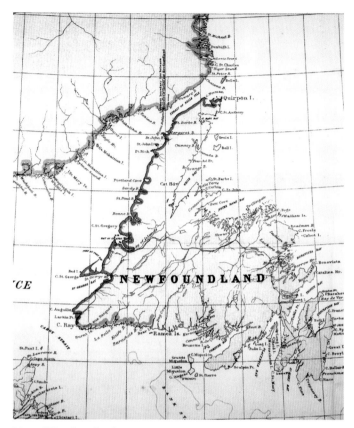

Map of Newfoundland, *c.* 1910.

American schooners and set the fish free. After this they cut up the Americans' nets and threw them away.

Another American herring ship, the *Moses Adams*, faired a bit better that day. Armed with revolvers, the captain and crew hastily scooped the herring from the nets, loaded them onto smaller boats and transported them back to the *Moses Adams*. By threatening to shoot any rioters who tried to stop them, the men of the *Moses Adams* managed to secure some of their catch. Eventually, the emboldened Canadians ripped the seine nets and allowed the remaining fish to escape.

Jubilant, the Newfoundland fishermen returned to shore and celebrated long into the night, shouting, blowing horns and firing guns. They had taken a stand and won the Fortune Bay Riot. The Americans had little doubt that the fishermen would do the same again. Fearing another incursion, the next day the American herring fleet headed home. But victory would be brief for Newfoundland. The American fishermen would persevere and continue to catch herring in these waters for decades to come.

In addition to battling Canadians, Americans fought among each other over herring. In 1806 citizens of Falmouth, Massachusetts, waged war against three mills on the Coona-messett River. Claiming that these mills had ruined their local herring fishery, the townspeople attempted to revoke the mills' privileges and remove some of their structures along the river. Infuriated by these moves, their opponents struck back by filling a cannon on the town green with herring and lighting it. Rather than spraying the townspeople with dead fish, the cannon exploded, killing the man who had lit it. Even after this tragedy, conflicts between industrialists and fishery advocates in Falmouth continued.

The fights over herring have yet to end. As recently as February 2015, scientists, fishermen and indigenous tribes in British Columbia clashed with the Canadian government over its move to open herring roe fisheries. Fuelling this fight is the Pacific herring's already compromised population. The three unlikely allies agreed that it would be foolhardy to allow open season on spawning herring. If the stock shrank further, so too would the region's population of seabirds, seals, whales and bears, all of which feast on the small fish. Animals such as humpback whales, which, until the late 1960s, were hunted almost to extinction and still remain a threatened species, would see their population recovery thwarted. The herring themselves could be annihilated forever.

Taking a page from the Newfoundland fishermen's book, in 2014 native people along British Columbia's coast prepared to take to the water and physically block the presence of industrial fisheries. A few applied for and received federal court injunctions to stop the fisheries. In response the government sent in the Royal Canadian Mounted Police to quell any interference with mass scale fishing. Ultimately, the government backed down but in 2015 the argument over whether or not to open roe fisheries began again.

While Canadian citizens endeavoured to save herring, on the other side of the globe the citizens of the Danish protectorate the Faroe Islands were busy defying regulations that protected herring. At issue were the European Union's herring quotas. The islanders asserted that they should be allotted more herring than other countries, for there were more fish in their waters. The Faroes have a population of less than 50,000 and are allowed roughly 5 per cent of the Atlantic herring catch.

Violating fishery management rules, in March 2013 the Faroe Islands brought in three times their allocated amount of herring, over 105,000 tons. At that time the combined weight permitted for all involved parties – Iceland, Norway, Russia, the Faroe Islands and the European Union – was 619,000 tons. Consequently, the European Union slapped sanctions on the Faroes. From August 2013 until August 2014 the Faroes were prohibited from exporting herring and mackerel to EU countries. Furthermore, their ships could not enter any EU ports with herring on board.

At times, herring played only a minor role in conflicts. Even so, battles were named for it. Such is the case with the fifteenth-century Battle of the Herrings near Rouvray, France. In February 1429, during the Hundred Years War, England sent five hundred cartloads of cannons, cannonballs, crossbows and herring to troops attacking the French garrison at Orléans. Three hundred of these carts were dedicated to salted herring. Lent was fast approaching and there was a tremendous need for preserved fish.

On the morning of 12 February 1429 the French and their Scottish allies came upon the English convoy near Rouvray in northern France. They attempted to capture the convoy and defeat the small army. In spite of the French army's size advantage, their Scottish allies made a gross tactical error, charging forward on foot when they should not have dismounted and broken rank. The men met bloodshed and carnage from the bows of English archers. Ultimately, the French and remaining Scots were forced to flee, thus losing the Battle of the Herrings. While the altercation was not officially fought over herring, it will forever be remembered in association with this fish.

Although at times it has been the cause of war, herring has also performed constructive roles in and immediately after wartime. During the First and Second World Wars countries encouraged their citizens to eat more fish and vegetables so that meat products could be sent to the troops. Forced to ration food, they handed out ration books so that their citizens could acquire an allotted number of necessities. Herring was among these essentials.

During the First World War American magazines such as *Good Housekeeping* offered domestic food conservation recipes. Among the dishes tested and approved by the Good Housekeeping Institute for 'their adaptability to wartime economy and food conservation' was moulded fish. This unusual-sounding repast consisted of a can of herring, a can of tuna, a stick of butter, a cup of stock, two tablespoons of

Second World War poster printed in Canada encouraging women to buy only what they need and continue rationing food.

Advertisement in the *Canadian Grocer* for Wallace's Herrings in Tomato Sauce, *c.* 1919.

gelatin, a dash of lemon juice and a pinch of paprika. Run through a food processor, spooned into a mould and then chilled, the disparate ingredients transformed into a hearty, savoury, high-calorie meal.

Because herring was such a staple of Second World War diets, it risked becoming mundane, if not dreaded. To keep cooks inspired and consumers satisfied, the UK Ministry of Food handed out flyers containing herring recipes. Included among the suggested dishes were mock fish cakes, which substituted herring paste for fish fillets, grilled herring, baked herring, oatmeal-crusted herring and potato salad with herring. In Norway cooks were instructed on how to make the national dish of lamb and cabbage stew, *fårikål*, with salted herring instead of lamb.

During this era all parts of herring were utilized. The roe appeared in dishes such as soft roe with baked spuds in jackets and herring-roe bread pudding. Regarding the latter, the Norwegian information office admitted that the dish sounded terrible but that 'it tastes almost like a good bread pudding'. Granted, this was far from a ringing endorsement but keep in mind that this was wartime and food, whether sweet, savoury or delectable, was scarce.

In the years after the Second World War Europe continued to suffer a paucity of food. Too many fields and crops had been destroyed. Too many animals had been killed. Too many labourers were lost at war. As a result, animal proteins were rare. To aid the hungry, a surfeit of canned herring were shipped and distributed as relief supplies, and to help tired cooks, herring recipes continued to appear in print. In her 1951 cookbook *French Country Cooking* the British food writer Elizabeth David offered a quick, easy and inexpensive way to prepare the fish: stuff the herring with a purée of potatoes, pepper, nutmeg and herbs and bake or grill the fish for 10 minutes. To jazz up cheap, plentiful herring roe, David advised covering the roe with chopped tomatoes, a strip of lemon zest, parsley, salt, pepper, butter and breadcrumbs and baking the ingredients for ten minutes. These and other creative recipes made the post-war herring provisions more palatable.

Often the tinned herring came from Iceland. During herring's prime it accounted for between 25 and 45 per cent of this Nordic island's export income. In the First and Second World Wars and the rough years following these wars, Iceland shipped enormous quantities of herring to Sweden, Finland, Denmark, the Soviet Union, Germany and the United States. It has been said that without herring and the jobs and wealth that they created, Iceland as we know it today would never have existed.

Herring fed the hungry. Herring fleets and fishermen defended them. In some lands, such as the Netherlands, herring ships played an integral part in establishing a national navy. In others, such as Great Britain, the fishing trawlers and their fishermen became part of the navy during wartime. Such was the case in England during both world wars.

Conscripted into the Royal Naval Patrol Service, British herring trawlers, with their pre-war crews at the helms, patrolled harbours, carried supplies and swept for mines. To convert the fishing vessel into a minesweeper, the trawler's net was replaced with a mine sweep. Sweep in place, the search for mines took place in the shipping lanes of British ports. The trawlers also erected boom defences, which are chains, nets, walls or other obstacles that block the movement of ships or submarines. These stop enemy vessels from gaining access to specific waterways or ports. Additionally, the trawlers transported fuel. Dubbed 'Essos' after the fuel of the same name, they were present during the 1944 invasion of Normandy.

Of the 1,637 British trawlers and other small civilian boats requisitioned during the Second World War, approximately 260 were destroyed. Even greater were the lives lost in the Royal Naval Patrol Service. Roughly 15,000 RNPS members were killed from the period of 1939 to 1945. Almost 2,400 of these men died at sea.

5
Away from European Shores

No one would argue that herring has played a fundamental part in the making, and occasional unmaking, of European nations. You cannot talk about the history of Amsterdam, Great Yarmouth, Scotland or Scandinavia without mentioning herring. Its reach, though, extends far beyond European shores, leaving an indelible mark upon the history of North America as well as Northeast Asia.

For millennia the indigenous people of North America's Pacific Northwest have lived and worked alongside herring. For at least 4,000 years the Tlingit of southeast Alaska and the Haida of Alaska and British Columbia have caught and consumed fresh herring. They have incorporated its oil into soaps. They have dried its roe on kelp or the branches of hemlock trees and later feasted on this delicacy.

The use of the entire fish began as a means of survival. To get by, people ate everything that was remotely edible. While subsistence living may no longer be the norm, herring remain an integral part of aboriginal life. Today tribes continue to fish, salt and smoke or pickle herring. They also dry or cook the roe.

Despite efforts to keep their herring traditions alive and the herring stock intact, Native Americans have repeatedly experienced threats to the population and health of this fish. Starting in the late nineteenth century, European settlers in the Pacific Northwest began opening commercial fisheries devoted to herring. Initially conservative with their hauls, the settlers' early enterprises salted and distributed roughly 13,600 kg (30,000 lb) of herring per year. After the First World War this number shot up to 12.7 million kg (28 million lb) per year.

By the 1930s the Pacific Northwest fisheries were culling an unsustainable 115 million kg (250 million lb) of herring every year. Much of the fish went to reduction plants, which turned the precious seafood into fertilizer, fish meal and oil. From 1926 to 1966, 90 per cent of southeast Alaska's herring catch ended up there.

In 1939 Alaskans started witnessing a severe drop in the herring population. That year the Bureau of Commercial Fisheries attempted to pinpoint where the schools in southeast Alaska had gone. Failing to locate the fish, the Bureau restricted the commercial fishing of herring to those caught for bait. By 1943 catch quotas had been established. Even so, at 12,500 tons (25 million pounds) per year, the limits did not seem all that restrictive.

After years of fluctuating herring populations and shifting quotas, in 1959 the state of Alaska stepped in and began to manage the fisheries. Seven years later the last reduction plant in the state closed. Market conditions and the decimated fish population were cited as the reasons for shutting the plants.

Alaskans didn't abandon fishing completely. Instead they turned their attention to herring roe. In the 1960s roe fisheries began popping up around the coast. The first focused on cultivating the eggs that had been laid on natural kelp beds. The fisheries later erected kelp-laden longlines in spawning areas and man-made kelp ponds. Because Pacific Northwest tribes such as the Haida and Tlingit relied upon roe as a food source, provisions were made to protect native fishing grounds from commercial harvesting.

The next decade saw a change in the direction of roe fisheries. Instead of taking the less destructive route of collecting roe that had already been laid, fishermen began removing the egg sac from female herring. This was done right before they spawned, when over 10 per cent of their body weight was comprised of roe.

The primary market for sac roe fisheries was Japan. By the 1970s Japan's supply of herring, and by default herring roe, had declined. To meet demands, the country began importing these delicacies from the Pacific Northwest. Although the increased interest in *Clupea pallasii*, the scientific name for Pacific herring, was a boon to North American fishermen, it put further pressure on an already compromised species. Stressed by overfishing, loss of habitat and sundry other factors, the herring population of Juneau, Alaska, collapsed in 1982. By 1993 the herring of Prince William Sound had

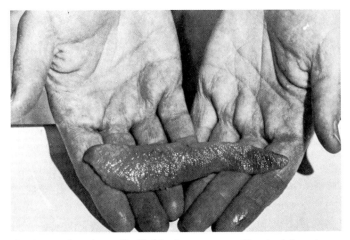

Herring roe from the u.s. Pacific Northwest was considered a delicacy in Japan and would bring in as much as $7 a pound in the 1940s.

followed suit. Alaskan herring weren't the only casualties. From 1973 to 2015 Washington state saw its herring population decline by 90 per cent. What fish remain are smaller and live half as long as their ancestors. Yet in spite of the lawsuits filed and fishery overhauls proposed by native Alaskans and Canadians, sac roe fisheries continue in the Pacific Northwest.

Further aggravating the herring's plight is pollution. Nothing has sullied the waters of the Northwest Pacific more than the disastrous *Exxon Valdez* oil spill. On 24 March 1989 the *Exxon Valdez* oil tanker struck Bligh Reef on Prince William Sound. Over the next several days the 240,000-freight ton ship dumped at least 11 million gallons of crude oil into the Sound's pristine waters. Until 2010's *Deepwater Horizon* catastrophe, this was the largest oil spill in American waters. It remains one of the most destructive, man-made environmental disasters on record.

Initially, scientists had predicted that the damage wrought by the *Exxon Valdez* would be tremendous but short-lived. Wildlife would die off but would rebound as the years passed and the fallout from the contamination dissipated. Instead, over 25 years later, ducks, otters, whales and herring continue to feel the impact.

Herring are alerted in scientists to the spill's long-term effects. As expected, no herring spawn survived the 1989 spill. By the spring of 1990 it seemed that the region's Pacific herring population had recovered. However, in 1993, it collapsed. That year the annual herring harvest was only 14 per cent of 1992's yield.

If this low figure wasn't disturbing enough, scientists noted that fish were dying midstream. Research conducted by the National Oceanic and Atmospheric Administration pointed to a reduction in the herring's ability to withstand prolonged swimming. It also noted a change in the shape of the fish's heart. These alterations, scientists hypothesized, came about as a result of the eggs' and larvae's exposure to a specific class of chemicals, polycyclic aromatic hydrocarbon, or PAH, found in crude oil. Tests would prove that PAH interferes with the electrical signals sent to the heart, causing it to slow down and/or stop. Hence herring exposed to residual oil were unable to swim as fast or far, or for as long.

These heart abnormalities, as well as weakened immune systems, meant that fewer herring made it to adulthood. If they did, their lives could still be shortened by cardiac complications. They could also be affected by viral haemorrhagic septicaemia or *Icthyophonus hoferi* infection, two diseases that have ravaged the herring of Prince William Sound.

Some scientists postulate that a recovered humpback whale, otter or seabird community has kept the herring numbers low. More hungry whales, otters and seabirds result in more luscious herring eaten. Whichever the cause, the Exxon Valdez Oil Spill Trustee Council classifies herring in the Sound as not having recovered from the effects of the 1989 spill.

Further down the Pacific Coast herring have fared better. With all the attention paid to its larger relation *Sardinia caerulea*, or the sardine, herring in the San Francisco Bay area have avoided overfishing. While Monterey's famed Cannery Row processed 332,000 tons of sardines every year from 1936 to 1945, herring slipped past the fishery nets. When California's sardine population shrank, herring briefly stepped in as a substitute for canned sardines. It did not take off with consumers as had been hoped and the demand for herring diminished. So, too, did the catches. In 1964 Bay area fishermen landed only 30,000 pounds of the fish.

Today San Francisco Bay is the largest herring mating grounds south of British Columbia. The fish arrive in late autumn and potter about until the combination of water temperature and salinity, substrate and absence of predators kicks off the spawn. This usually occurs in late December or early January.

The ritual begins with the males releasing their milt and pheromones. This alerts the females that their job is about to start. The female herring then lay their adhesive eggs on rocks, pilings, riprap and seaweed. The California Department of Fish and Wildlife has reported as much as 30 km of shoreline blanketed by 10-metre swathes of herring eggs.

Many eggs are picked off by hordes of gulls, pelicans, cormorants and ducks. Frenzied birds are said to dive by the tens of thousands to grab herring eggs. Birds aren't the only threats. Seals, sea lions, porpoises, dolphins and larger fish vie for these protein-rich treats. So, too, do commercial fishermen who closely follow the November to March runs.

During the 2014 spawning season there were an estimated 60,600 tons of Pacific herring bustling about in the Bay. Each year the California Department of Fish and Wildlife sets a new quota for herring. In 2015, 2,302 tons of herring and roe were taken while in 2014 it was 3,737 tons. The fishing season extends through March or until the quota is met.

Typically, herring from the Bay is caught for its roe with Japan as the intended market. In Japan it appears in a traditional caviar dish called *kazunoko kombu*. Served at New Year's celebrations, this speciality consists of herring eggs seasoned with seaweed or dashi kombu, soy sauce and savoury broth made from dried bonito flakes. *Kazunoko kombu* is said to symbolize fertility and prosperity in the coming year.

Like other lands, Japan has a complicated relationship with herring. Since at least the fifteenth century the Japanese have fished for *nishin* or herring. Most people catch *nishin* off the coast of Hokkaido in the Sea of Japan. Here, along the

Herring sushi artfully prepared in Tokyo, Japan.

country's northernmost island, herring have two spawning seasons, from late January to early May and from August to December.

By the end of the seventeenth century Hokkaido had established herring fisheries and begun to distribute dried herring and herring roe around the country. The fish starred in *nishin soba*, marinated herring served atop soba noodles; *nishin-tsuke*, herring simmered in a sugar, salt and soy sauce; *nishin no shioyaki*, salt-broiled herring; and grilled dried herring. It also appeared in the fish and winter vegetable soup known as sanpei soup, tempura and sushi rolls.

Although they did eat herring, the Japanese more frequently turned their catches into fertilizer. In fact, by the 1940s only 30 per cent of the country's catch would be used for food. The rest would enrich cotton, tobacco and sundry other crops in southeastern Japan. In the nineteenth century the Hokkaido harbour city of Otaru grew out of the demand for herring meal. Today you can see remnants of its zenith in the *nishin goten*, or herring mansions. Built for affluent fishermen, these palatial estates featured lacquered floors, hand-plastered walls and tile roofs. Although erected to house the newly wealthy, the mansions also served as fish processing plants and residences for the plant's employees.

In 1897 Hokkaido saw the greatest herring landing ever, with 975,000 tons of fish hauled in along its coastlines. By the late 1930s Japan, along with the United States and Canada, accounted for more than 50 per cent of world's total catch of herring and its allied species (into which category sardines, pilchards, anchovies and shad all fall). Catching and processing such an immense number of fish could only yield one thing – the herring supply was radically depleted. By 1958 Japan's fisheries had collapsed and the Hokkaido herring was said to be extinct.

Deprived of their own stock, Japanese fishing fleets set out for the Pacific Northwest and North America's herring. In the 1960s they brokered deals with British Columbia to set up fisheries in provincial waters. Problems arose when, instead

A 19th-century *nishin goten*, herring mansion, in Otaru, Japan.

of hiring Canadians, the Japanese imported labourers from home. In 1969 Canada's United Fishermen and Allied Workers' Union (UFAWU) tried and failed to stop the importation of Japanese workers. Nonetheless, the Canadian government continued to grant work permits to the Japanese. In 1970 Canada allowed the first Japanese herring roe fishery to open.

To save money, roe processing plants hired women. Women supposedly had nimbler fingers than men and therefore could extract the egg sacs more easily and quickly. They could also be paid less than their male counterparts. In many instances they received 77 per cent of what male employees earned for the same work. Although the UFAWU raised this as another problem with Japanese companies, these businesses continued to thrive on Canadian shores.

By the late 1970s 80 per cent of Japan's herring roe was coming from British Columbia. The value of roe had skyrocketed. In 1978, 70,000 tons were harvested for an astonishing price of $53 million. While the following year yielded only 41,000 tons, it was worth $150 million, almost three times the previous year's catch. Profitability spurred the creation of additional fisheries. Officials in the Fisheries Association of British Columbia began to worry that the Japanese would control 90 per cent of the province's processing plants. By 1980, though, the roe market had collapsed. Eggs that had sold for $16 per pound were now going for $6. The 1980 catch was valued at $10 million.

This crisis brought an end to rampant Japanese involvement with British Columbia's herring. Instead, the Japanese turned their attention back to their own shores and to improving their herring supply. The 1980s saw the introduction of a herring nursery in Hokkaido. Still in operation, this population enhancement programme involves the collection of milt and roe from wild-caught herring. The belief is that wild fish will produce more genetically varied and hardy offspring.

At the nursery eggs are fertilized and placed in filtered, aerated and temperature-controlled seawater. There they incubate for roughly 150 days. Right before hatching, the eggs are moved to tanks where the water temperature is slowly raised to 15°C (59°F). After hatching, the larvae are fed formula; they will receive this special food until six months of age. At two months the fry move out of their tanks and into pens. This is where they become accustomed to a more natural environment. At this point copepods and crustacean larvae are introduced to their diet, further acclimating them to life outside the hatchery. Just before being released, they are marked with fluorescent labels so that scientists can monitor them in the wild.

Managed by the Japan Aquaculture Association, the herring nursery programme produces at least one million fry per year. Out of that million, only 40 per cent survive long enough to be released into the sea. Researchers have cited egg source, a failure to adapt to a new diet, poor nutrition and the lethalness of chemicals used in labelling as possible causes of premature death. But in spite of the high mortality rate, nursery-raised juveniles have boosted Japan's herring population. There has been a slow increase from 1,366 tons caught in 2002 to approximately 4,500 tons in 2013. The programme seems to be gradually advancing the health and sustainability of herring.

On the other side of the globe, in the North Atlantic, herring has had just as raucous a history. In 1622 a Virginian official named John Pory wrote an account of his visit to Plymouth, Massachusetts, and of seeing

> another kind of fish which they call herring, or old wives, in infinite schools into a small river running under the town, and so into a great pond or lake of a

mile broad where they cast their spawn, the water of the said river being in many places not above half a foot deep. Yea, when a heap of stones is reared up against them a foot high above the water, they leap and tumble over and will not be beaten back with cudgels.

With that last notion Pory coined a catchphrase that has lasted for centuries. Herein rests the origins of the popular saying 'beating them back with a stick'. Later in his recounting Pory described how Plymouth residents utilized the fish that swam up the Town Brook and into Billington Sea to spawn each spring.

The inhabitants during the said two months take them up every day in hogsheads, and with those they eat not they manure the ground, burying 2 or 3 in each hill of corn, and may, when they are able, if they see cause, lade whole ships with them. At their going up they are very fat and savory, but at their coming down, after they have cast their spawn, they are shot, and therefore lean and unwholesome.

If not every American, then every resident of Plymouth has heard the story of the Native American Squanto teaching the seventeenth-century Plymouth settlers how to grow corn. To achieve a successful crop, the Patuxet tribesman instructed the colonists to plant dead herring alongside each seed in a method known as 'spot fertilizing'. The decomposing herring fertilized the plantings. Their calcium- and lime-rich bones also neutralized the sandy and acidic soil.

Although only corn was spot fertilized with herring, it remained an invaluable tool for the fledgling farmers. With it the pilgrims were able to grow fields of healthy Indian corn (maize). When farmers didn't having herring or enough of it, they would claim this as the reason for a failed crop.

To stock up on herring and ensure good plantings, people installed weir traps in their local rivers. Unfortunately, it was illegal for them to set their own traps and take what was considered communal fish. Such was the case in 1632 in Watertown, Massachusetts, where immigrants set up unauthorized weirs in the Charles River. Facing punishment, they justified their actions by stating that their crops had fallen short the previous year 'for want of fish'.

Despite illicit fish trapping the area's herring supply remained strong. In fact, the plethora of herring astounded the pilgrims. In 1634 William Wood wrote in *New England's Prospect* that herring arrived 'in such multitudes as is almost incredible, pressing up such shallow waters as will scarce permit them to swim'. Some colonists noted that, by damming a river with a few stones, a fisherman could capture several thousand herring without the use of traps. Others wrote of adults and children catching fish with their bare hands.

So important was herring to this region that the first fishery law drafted in Plymouth observed, 'God by his providence hath cast the fish called alewives or herrings in the midst of the place appointed for the town of Plymouth.' Other documents similarly discussed divine providence having a hand in the bounty of herring that was conveniently available to settlers in need of nourishment.

Plymouth wasn't the only settlement to benefit from herring. Across New England people were cultivating healthy corn crops and weathering tough winters with their cache of preserved herring. It seemed to be the fish of unlimited uses and supply.

History reminds us again and again that, if copious quantities of a beneficial resource exist, man will exploit them until little is left. It happened to herring in Europe, Asia and the Pacific Northwest, and it eventually occurred in Colonial America, too. Breaching agreements made with the Native Americans, colonists erected dams, weir traps and water mills on indigenous fishing grounds. They organized commercial fisheries and started a privatization of the herring market. Once people started thinking of herring as an indispensable agricultural tool, prices rose. With that, so did the number of people poaching it.

In communities where everyone was apportioned a share of the catch, herring agents became common. These men did everything from distributing fish and collecting payments to guarding traps and stopping poachers. In 1696 officials in Middleborough, Massachusetts, wrote of their intention for herring agents 'to use all lawful means for the taking of the fish for the benefit of the whole town'.

Not every agent worked within the law or for the good of the community. Money went missing. Allotments meant to be equal varied in size. Some shares disappeared altogether. The latter happened when unscrupulous agents collected fees from the villagers, packed up the fish and then re-sold it elsewhere. During this period sales of black market herring flourished.

Whether the offender was a townsperson or an agent, those caught breaking the law could be placed in the stocks for 24 hours. If they didn't end up in the stocks, they could be lashed five times with a whip or imprisoned for a day. Restitution also had to be paid. Punishments applied to children as well as adults. Even with these penalties, the crimes continued. By the early eighteenth century northeastern Massachusetts reported a dearth of herring. Dams, weirs and mills were cited as the causes for the fish's absence. In this part of the state it had been fished or forced out of its home.

Massachusetts wasn't the only New England state to live through the rise and fall of herring. In the nineteenth century America's easternmost town and first major port, Lubec, Maine, became a hub for herring smoking. By 1831 Lubec boasted twenty smokehouses curing between 2,000 and 3,000 barrels of fish each year. The small fishing villages of Steuben and Millbridge soon joined Lubec in smoking fish. Within ten years Maine was shipping nearly a half million boxes of smoked herring a year to such East Coast cities as Boston, New York and Philadelphia.

Besides smoking herring, Mainers put the fish into cans. Lubec's and Eastport's canneries packaged small, whole, immature herring in tins and sold them as sardines. The masquerade was an attempt to compete with European-sourced sardines. The ruse proved so successful that it continued into the twenty-first century.

The first step in the herring's path to becoming a tinned sardine was to be beheaded and gutted. It was then washed and salted or pickled. This accomplished, the fish was placed on a wire frame known as a flake. This frame held the herring in place as it rotated through a hot oven. After fifteen to thirty minutes the fish had finished cooking and was removed and cooled on a rack. This cooling rack and dozens like it were taken to a packing room, where the fish were placed in cans containing vegetable oil. The oil kept the fish moist and preserved. The tins of fish were then sealed and tested to ensure that no leaks existed.

Entire families worked at the canneries. Fathers and sons cleaned and cooked the fish while the women and girls packed them into cans. The men finished the process by sealing the tins.

Scads of northeast coast towns owed their burgeoning communities to herring fishing and canning. Eastport, Maine, was one such place. In 1840 it had a population of around 2,800. By 1890 this number had nearly doubled.

Perhaps more impressive was the number of canneries that the small town of Eastport maintained. The first opened in 1875. Ten years later, thirteen more were in operation. By the turn of the twentieth century Maine had 75 fish canneries, twenty of which were based in Eastport.

Life in Maine during the late nineteenth and early twentieth century seemed charmed. Herring and herring-related jobs were plentiful. Two world wars, each requiring portable, long-lasting foods, kept the canneries busy and profitable. Overall, the populace was thriving. Things, though, were about to change. In the mid-twentieth century foreign fishing fleets entered the Northeast Atlantic and began landing record hauls. Until the 1950s the region's annual herring catches had weighed 66,000 metric tons. By 1968 this number had skyrocketed to 470,000 metric tons. As a result of this unsustainable harvesting, New England's herring fisheries collapsed. Things only got bleaker from there.

Between the crash of the fisheries and Americans developing a taste for canned tuna, New England's canneries either closed or started processing other foods. By 2001 the last canning plant in Lubec had shut its doors. Lubec's remaining commercial smokehouse had closed eleven years earlier. In April 2010 Maine's final sardine cannery ceased to operate. And yet, North Atlantic herring fisheries persist. In 1976 Congress passed the Magnuson-Stevens Act to control u.s. fishery management. Also known as the Fishery Conservation and Management Act of 1976, it implemented the protection of fish habitat, reduction of by-catch and conservation of resources. Foreign fishing was phased out and domestic fisheries became regulated. Slowly, the herring population recovered.

Atlantic herring is no longer considered overfished or at risk. Nonetheless, it continues to be managed through annual catch limits and fishery closures. In 2015 the National Marine Fisheries Service shut down the Gulf of Maine herring fishery for half the year. It warned seafood dealers not to accept any Atlantic herring caught during this time. These moves were made to ensure that stocks remained robust and the fishery didn't go beyond its catch limit.

Exceeding catch quotas is an ongoing concern. In 2014 trawlers towing football-field-sized nets off the coast of Cape Cod pulled in so much herring that they surpassed the regional limit by 60 per cent. This happened at the start of the fishing season, causing further alarm among the fishing community. By depleting the amount of forage fish available, these trawlers may have driven away valuable predatory fish such as striped bass and bluefin tuna. The trawlers also reduced the bait supply for lobster fishermen and of fish for human consumption. Care must be taken to stop further infractions against the herring population in the Atlantic and the Pacific Oceans, otherwise there may be no herring left.

6

Fish Meal and Fertilizer

The thought of taking a nutrient-filled, flavourful fish and turning it into a processed food for plants and other fish may sound like a waste of good seafood. Yet for centuries man has done that very thing, converting herring into such mass-produced items as fish meal, oil, bait and fertilizer.

By definition 'fish meal' refers to fish or fish waste that has been dried out and ground into a powder. This powder is fed to poultry, pigs, farmed fish and pets. Fish meal is touted as offering a balanced dose of essential amino acids, minerals, phospholipids and fatty acids. These help increase growth rates and overall yields of animals and fish. Furthermore, proponents claim that farmed fish absorb the nutrients in fish meal more efficiently. This, in turn, decreases water pollution levels. In the world of aquaculture, pollution is an obvious and ongoing concern.

A form of fish meal has existed since at least the thirteenth century. In *The Travels of Marco Polo* Polo wrote of his journey through Yemen and of watching farmers feeding their livestock dried fish:

> These people are great fishermen . . . They dry them in the sun, and as by reason of the extreme heat, the country

is in a manner burnt up, and no sort of vegetable is to be seen, they accustom their cattle, cows, sheep, camels, and horses to feed upon dried fish, which being regularly served to them, they eat without any signs of dislike. The fish used for this purpose are of a small kind, which they take in vast quantities during the moths of March, April, and May; and when dried, they lay up in their houses for the food of their cattle.

Polo calls this fish 'tunny' or tuna. Based on his description of the animal fodder and on species lists from the Gulf of Aden and Arabian Sea, the small fish was probably a member of the Clupeidae family. Polo could have meant sardines or round herring. While herring-like in appearance and in name, the tiny round herring belongs to the Dussumieriidae and not the Clupeidae family.

In scorching, sun-drenched countries, fish were dried outdoors. In cold, dreary lands people resorted to pressing fish. Ninth-century Norwegians squeezed whole herring between rocks and wood to remove the oil and dry out the flesh. Over a millennium later, this technique is still employed in the commercial production of fish meal.

Modern processors both dry and press fish. To create fish meal, plants use raw herring and other forage fish such as anchovies, menhaden and sardines. They also add in bones, skin and viscera from filleted fish. Placed on a conveyor belt, the fish and scraps glide through a steam cooker. They then travel through a perforated and pressurized tube that extracts oil and water. This liquid, known as press liquor, will be separated and processed so that the water and oil can be repurposed. At the end of the pressing stage the fish, or press cakes as they are now called, contain about 4 per cent oil and 50 per cent water. Because they still hold some moisture,

Fish from the Clupeidae family air-drying in Nazaré, Portugal.

The final product, mounds of North American-produced fish meal, *c.* 1979.

the press cakes must be dried, otherwise they will become rancid.

Drying is a tricky stage. If the press cakes become too parched, they will lose their nutritional value. If too much moisture is left behind, the cakes will breed mould and bacteria and become unsafe for consumption. To combat these issues, the press cakes undergo indirect or direct drying. In the latter case 500°C (930°F) air is blown over the cakes as they are tossed around in a drum. The searing hot air evaporates the water. With indirect drying the cakes are placed in a steam-jacketed cylinder or a cylinder with steam-heated discs. The cakes tumble about in the cylinder until dry. This is more or less the same process as in direct drying.

The last step is to grind the press cakes. Grinding breaks up bits of bone and other large particles in the cakes. The finished product is either stored in silos or bagged for distribution. Because of its low water content, fish meal does not need to be refrigerated.

As of 2010 roughly 6.3 million tons of fish meal and 1.1 million tons of fish oil were processed each year globally from 33 million tons of fish and fish trimmings. Presently, Peru is the greatest producer of fish meal and oil. Chile, China and the Nordic countries of Denmark, Norway and Iceland are the next top five producers.

According to a report from the Food and Agricultural Organization of the United Nations, in 2014 Germany, the United Kingdom and the United States represented the largest growing markets for fish meal. This growth was due to aquaculture and terrestrial farming demands for the product. At 2 million metric tons, China is the biggest annual consumer of fish meal. Japan, Thailand and Norway are the next. Even so, they lag behind China at a paltry 0.7 million metric tons of meal imported each year.

u.s. salmon cannery and herring reduction plant.

Remember press liquor, the liquid consisting of oil, water and dissolved proteins, minerals and vitamins that was extracted in the production of fish meal? After being collected, these liquids are separated from each other. To accomplish this, the press liquor is sent through a centrifuge. The oil, which has risen to the top, is skimmed off and set aside. The leftover water and soluble nutrients, dubbed 'stickwater', are cooked down until the liquid becomes thick and syrupy and includes between 40 and 50 per cent of solid matter. Once the proper consistency has been achieved, the stickwater is added to the press cake. The cake is then dried and ground into fish meal.

While the liquids and soluble nutrients are converted into stickwater, the remaining fish oil runs through a second centrifuge. This filters out any remaining solids and impurities. The refined oil is then pumped into storage tanks. Like fish meal, fish oil is used to feed omnivorous farmed fish such as trout and salmon.

Fish aren't the only creatures dipping into the fish oil supply. If you've ever seen a bottle of amber capsules claiming to be chock-full of omega-3 fatty acids at a pharmacy, market or healthfood store, you've encountered fish oil manufactured from herring and sundry pelagic fish. Falling into the broad category of nutraceuticals, fish oil supplements contain a trace amount of vitamin E to prevent spoilage. They may also have calcium, iron or vitamins A, B, C or D added to them.

Consumers are wild about these gelatin capsules. According to a July 2015 article in *The Independent*, in the 1990s fish oil sales were in the tens of millions of dollars. So far, in the twenty-first century, Americans have spent roughly $1.2 billion annually on fish oil pills and related supplements.

Fish oil is seen as a panacea for a host of ailments, including the obvious cardiovascular issues such as high blood

An abundance of fish oil capsules.

pressure, high cholesterol, heart disease and stroke. People pop the capsules to combat such disparate afflictions as asthma, osteoporosis, psoriasis, glaucoma, obesity, inflammation, pain, depression, dyslexia and hyperactivity. In spite of their popularity the merits of fish oil supplements remain questionable.

Omega-3 fatty acids are what fish oil proponents seek. The human body doesn't produce omega-3 fatty acids, nor can it convert omega-6 fatty acids into omega-3s. Yet omega-3s are important to overall wellness and play a role in brain function and the aforementioned cardiovascular health. They also decrease pain, inflammation and the risk of blood clots. Those who don't like oily, omega-3 rich fish but are concerned about their health are among the multitudes reaching for fish oil pills.

Considering how popular herring is with larger, predatory fish, it should come as no surprise that fishermen cash in on this attraction and bait their hooks with herring. As bait, herring attracts such coveted quarry as salmon, cod, striped bass, snapper, haddock and halibut. Its silvery skin and oily scent lure such crustaceans as shrimp, lobster and crab.

To procure live herring for bait, you could try the Native American approach known as torching. With this technique a torch or small metal basket filled with birch bark is placed at the bow of a small fishing boat. Set ablaze, the torch's light draws in the herring. Wielding hand-held dip nets, fishermen scoop up the fish that mill around their boat and put them in buckets. On a good night, over the course of several hours, they may net several thousand fish.

Alternatively, you can fish for herring. Special rigs, known as sabiki rigs or bait catchers, will pull in several herring at a time. These rigs consist of multiple small hooks, each of which possess an individual line. Because the various hooks and lines tend to get tangled up in each other, sabiki rods, crafted

New England fishermen torching with a floating lantern, *c.* 1877.

expressly for sabiki rigs, have become popular with herring fishermen. You can still fish with your regular rod, too.

If you don't want to mess around with hooking live fish, you can purchase frozen bait at bait shops and from online purveyors. It comes either vacuum-packed or as one giant block of fish. To turn herring into frozen bait, fishermen dump their herring catches into holding pens. There they deprive the fish of food so that their fat content decreases. Less fat means firmer flesh that keeps its shiny scales. These scales make herring more enticing to other fish. Once the herring have reached the desired weight and appearance, they are killed, frozen and sold.

After acquiring herring bait, fishermen might cut the fish into little pieces. These small bites attract smaller fish. If aiming for substantial-sized fish, they either slice the herring into large strips or thread whole herring onto their hooks. Before baiting the hook, they take a sharp knife and slash the herring's sides. These cuts release the fish's scent and increase the desirability of the bait.

Along with acting as bait, herring has one other, rather unglamorous job: that of fertilizer. Around the time that Squanto was showing the English colonists how to fertilize corn with fish, Japanese farmers were enriching their fields with herring. During the Edo period of 1603 to 1868 Japan's demand for herring-based fertilizer blossomed as commercial farmers increasingly depended on it for their rice and cotton crops. Known as *nishin shimekasu*, the fertilizer consisted of boiled, pressed herring. Produced in Hokkaido, *nishin shimekasu* routinely made its way south to Japan's main island of Honshu. On Honshu farmers used it to grow rice. After harvesting their crops, the farmers shipped the rice back to Hokkaido where it was either consumed or made into rice wine. Herring travelled back and forth from

Atlantic herring.

Hokkaido and Honshu in some form or another for hundreds of years.

Prior to the introduction of *nishin shimekasu* Japanese farmers had fertilized their plants with expensive and scarce dried sardines. Low in cost and abundant in number, herring quickly supplanted sardines as the favoured fertilizer. According to David Luke Howell in *Capitalism from Within: Economy, Society, and the State in a Japanese Fishery* (1995), by the twentieth century herring outsold dried sardine fertilizer in Japan by fourteen to one.

Wherever there was a surplus of herring, there was herring fertilizer. During the eighteenth and nineteenth century New England farmers were encouraged to put it on their fields. This suggestion came, in part, from the huge number of herring being caught by East Coast fishermen. The supply exceeded the demand. People had no choice but to spread the unwanted herring onto pastures and plough them into the land. To this end, agricultural journals began touting the value of herring for enriching the soil. One nineteenth-century publication, *DeBow's Review*, claimed that one medium-sized fish rivalled the quality of a large shovelful of manure. Another boasted of the amazing results gained by an Englishman who tilled his land with 32,000 fish.

Living next to thousands of decomposing fish may sound like a smelly proposition. This is one of the downsides to herring fertilizer. The stench is unavoidable. So, too, are the creatures attracted by the odour. Old farm journals overflow with complaints of crows unearthing and consuming herring almost immediately after the fish had been buried. Dogs, pigs and other four-legged creatures posed the same problem. To stop the thieving and protect the crops, children were enlisted to chase away invaders. Even with these young guards in place, the wildlife managed to abscond with fish.

Although far fewer people stick whole, dead herring into the ground today, gardeners continue to feed their plants with fish fertilizer or fish protein hydrolysates. To craft this compost, whole fish and fish scraps are broken down by naturally occurring enzymes. They are then mixed with a smidgen of phosphoric acid, which controls the pH level. Fish protein hydrolysates claim not to smell as much as fish meal, whole fish or other fish fertilizers do.

7
What's Cooking
with Herring?

Much has been said of the Danish love of herring, particularly pickled herring. Yet Denmark is not alone in its adoration and creation of herring dishes. In addition to *böckling* pudding and the horrific-smelling *surströmming*, Sweden has *sotare* or grilled Baltic herring and *stekt inlagd strömming*, fried pickled herring. A part of Sweden's traditional Christmas smorgasbord, fried pickled herring feature a delicate breading of rye flour and breadcrumbs. After being pan-fried in salted butter, the fish is dressed with a light vinaigrette or diced onion.

Another Swedish gem is clay pot herring. This reinterpretation of the classic potato-onion-anchovy casserole Jansson's Temptation replaces the customary anchovies with herring. Herring partners with onion in another Scandinavian baked dish, *sillåda*, which is comprised of layers of herring and onion seasoned with allspice, ground ginger and chopped parsley. Topped with buttered breadcrumbs and baked until bubbling, it is another delicious one-pot meal.

In Finland herring plays a prominent part in holiday feasts. Like the Danes, Finns pickle herring, matching it with such colourful and aromatic ingredients as carrots, tomatoes, juniper berries and star anise. They may serve it plain or roll it into a *silakkarulla*, herring roulade. For *silakkarulla* you spread

Pickled herring sandwiches in Berlin.

a layer of breadcrumbs, herbs, cheese or ham over a herring fillet. Roll up the fillet, secure it with a skewer and bake it in a sauce of vinegar and tomatoes or seasoned cream. No Finnish Christmas dinner is complete without some form of *silliä* or pickled herring.

If you eat a lot of one specific food, chances are that you will devise a variety of ways to prepare it. Such is the case in Germany. In addition to rollmops and Bismarcks, herring appears in *Bratheringe*. Here, herring fillets are dredged in flour, fried in butter and marinated in a mixture of vinegar, sugar, water, mustard seeds and bay leaves. *Bratheringe* are served cold with bread and boiled or mashed potatoes.

Heringstopf mit saurer Sahne, or herring salad with sour cream, pairs herring with sour cream, yogurt or mayonnaise, sliced onions and apples. Another salad, *Heringsalat*, brings pickled herring together with beetroot, pickled gherkins, apples, roast beef, capers, vinegar and hardboiled eggs. Lightly tossed, herring salad is a German party regular.

Along with salads Germany has an array of simple but scrumptious herring sandwiches. Served on long rolls with lettuce and sliced onion or gherkins, peppers, tomatoes or a sprinkling of caviar or dill, they are a fixture at fairs, festivals and Oktoberfests. Washed down with a pint of Pilsner or Märzen, these sandwiches provide a pleasant alternative to the standard fried carnival fare.

In Russia herring appears in such appetizers as herring fritters, beer-battered herring, herring baked with ground beef and potatoes and rollmops. Generally, pickled herring is partnered with sour cream, horseradish, cabbage, beets, onion, gherkins or radishes. No Russian wedding, funeral or family party is complete without some type of herring on the table.

Although herring may hold more culinary heft on European shores, it does have North American fans. On the u.s. East Coast one cannot talk about herring without mentioning New York City's Russ & Daughters. In business on the Lower East Side for over a hundred years, the family-owned store specializes in foods to pair with bagels, including pickled herring. Dubbed 'the house that herring built', Russ & Daughters sells such standbys as pickled herring with onions, cream and onions, mustard and dill and curry as well as *matjes*, rollmops and schmaltz. Its nearby café serves

A pickled herring platter at New York's Russ & Daughters.

canapés of pickled herring, herring platters and schmaltz with a vodka shot.

As demonstrated by these distinct dishes, herring marries well with a host of ingredients. Allspice, bay leaf, coriander seed, dill, mustard, parsley, tarragon, pepper, salt, lemon, soy sauce, vinegar and white wine complement its oily flesh. Anchovies, apples, bacon, beetroot, breadcrumbs, butter, cream, eggs, garlic, fresh greens, onions, pickles and potatoes also partner nicely with it. A versatile fish, it can stand in for sardines, sprats and mackerel in recipes. Fresh herring can be pan-fried, grilled, baked, broiled or hot-smoked. It certainly can be pickled and salt-cured. If fresh, young herring are frozen first to kill off parasites, the fish can be consumed raw and put in sushi and ceviches.

Whole, fresh herring tastes fabulous when baked with a stuffing of breadcrumbs and chopped onion and apple or minced garlic, onions and parsley. It is superb wrapped in bacon and then grilled or broiled. Possessing an affinity for bacon, it does splendidly when rolled in oats and pan-fried in bacon fat.

If you are lucky enough to locate a fresh-off-the-boat, whole herring, you will need to do a little work before you can enjoy your fish. In essence, unless someone on the boat or at the port has scaled and gutted the herring for you, you'll have to clean it. Thankfully, this doesn't require much effort. The first step is to remove the scales. Holding the herring under cold, running water, brush the scales off with your fingers. They should slide gently off the fish. Any stubborn ones can be scraped off with a knife.

If your fish hasn't been gutted, you will do this next. Grab a sharp knife or pair of kitchen scissors and use it to slit open the herring's belly from the head almost to the tail. Pull out the innards and backbone and discard them. If you cannot snap off the head, cut it off with your knife or scissors. Rinse the fish under running water, brushing off any remaining scales or entrails. Once the fish has been washed a second time, your cleaning work is done. You can now preserve the fish in salt, pickle or smoke it, or grill, bake, fry or broil it. It's that easy.

Working with roe is even simpler. Herring roe has two primary preparations: baked and fried. In Scandinavian recipes it tends to be fried whole and paired with a rich sauce and potatoes or fried and eaten cold on an open-faced sandwich. In the UK it is fried in butter and served on hot buttered toast. It also turns up in such unusual places as curries and scrambled eggs. It serves as the roe in the Greek fish roe dip taramasalata and as caviar in Japanese *kazunoko kombu*.

Unlike traditional caviar, which has a buttery taste, the roe from herring imparts a subtle flavour. Pale yellow in colour, it has a somewhat gritty texture. Nevertheless, with authentic wild sturgeon caviar going for as much as $3,200 per pound, herring roe offers amazing value. Prices in 2015 ranged from $7 to $12 per pound. No need to question why people refer to this roe as 'poor man's caviar'.

With herring roe and the fish itself being such a bargain, you might expect more cooks to incorporate it into meals. Rather than helping its image, its inexpensiveness has hurt it. When your eggs are perceived as the underprivileged's caviar, your flesh tends to fall into a similar, lacklustre category. As a result, consumers often snub what, in recent history, has been nicknamed the food of the poor.

Considering the ongoing interest in omega-3 fatty acids and increasing concern for seafood sustainability, herring's standing may improve. Owing to its presence in such world-renowned restaurants as Copenhagen's Noma, it undoubtedly will experience a rise in public awareness and esteem.

Having people understand the nutritional and culinary values of herring is key. So is having more consumers recognize that there exists a delightful, small fish that goes by the name of herring. Helping in that quest for recognition are the European herring galas. As a tribute to the fish's role in their history, numerous European cities host multi-day events dedicated to herring.

In the Netherlands Vlaggetjesdag, or Flags' Day, kicks off the start of the new herring season. On that day in late May or early June throngs descend upon the Dutch port of Scheveningen to check out the local fishing boats and sample herring cures. Visitors can watch fish auctions and fish cleaning, filleting and cooking demonstrations, model ship building and vendors peddling the latest fishing equipment and gadgets. In keeping with a fair-like atmosphere, Flags' Day includes live music, arts and crafts, traditional Dutch fishing costumes and an abundance of herring.

While the Dutch Vlaggetjesdag became an official celebration in the late 1940s, Finland's Helsinki Baltic Herring
Fair has taken place since 1743. Held in October, the early
events performed a practical purpose. They gave Finns the
opportunity to stock up on herring for the brutal winter
months ahead. The week-long festival still occurs along the
Helsinki harbour, where fishermen bring their fresh catches
to *silakkamarkkinat*, the herring market. During the fair they
sell the fish directly from their boats. An assortment of fresh,
salted, pickled, smoked and fermented herring, brines and
marinades are available as well.

Denmark's Hvide Sande Herring Festival is all about
catching herring. Each spring Hvide-Sande hosts the country's
largest angling competition. The contestants' quarry is herring
migrating to the Ringkøbing Fjord to spawn. Along with fishing competitions, contestants challenge each other in herring
filleting, the best herring recipe and the race for the title of
'Mr Herring'. To win the last contest, fishermen dressed only
in waders prowl a catwalk and answer random questions posed

Bites of pickled herring.

by a panel of judges. Whoever garners the position of Mr Herring takes home cash and a new pair of waders.

On the northern coast of Iceland the fishing village of Siglufjörður embraces its past at an annual summer herring festival. Held in cooperation with Siglufjörður's Herring Era Museum, the commemoration includes pickling demonstrations, tastings and talks about when herring was king and the fishing industry was booming. Unfortunately, no herring remain around Siglufjörður, but the impact of the fish is still noted.

Not every country with a herring fete is Nordic. On the second Thursday in June Glückstadt in Germany kicks off Glückstädter Matjeswochen, a four-day celebration of the start of the new herring season. The yearly jubilee begins with a *matjes* tasting in the town's marketplace. Taken from a large wooden barrel, the fish is sampled by the mayor before being served to the crowd.

Each July the fishing community of Eyemouth, Scotland, crowns a herring queen at its annual Herring Queen Festival. The queen arrives by boat in Eyemouth Harbour and is accompanied to the swearing-in ceremony by the boat's skipper and a procession of attendants. After receiving her crown, the Herring Queen lays wreaths on the town's War Memorial and the Memorial to the Fishermen of Eyemouth. The latter honours the 189 fishermen lost at sea during an unexpected storm on 14 October 1881.

On the Devon coast the English village of Clovelly pays tribute with its yearly Herring Festival. Activities include net making, cooking demonstrations, tastings, photography exhibits on Clovelly herring fishing and maritime talks. Kippers and bloaters are smoked and consumed on site.

In recent years the United States has got in on the herring fun. Alaska's Sitka Herring Festival sponsors lectures on

A British-inspired way to enjoy pickled herring: in a tea sandwich.

herring conservation, fisheries, management and food culture. It also holds potlucks and hands-on demonstrations and screens movies about the fish.

Occurring in January, the Sausalito Herring Festival pays homage to the fish that helps to sustain San Francisco Bay's last commercial fishery. Throughout Massachusetts, fishing communities throw parties in honour of the annual spring herring run. Herring tastings and conservation talks are frequently on the schedule.

Functions such as these only increase the world's awareness of this historic little fish. Moreover, they educate consumers about nutritional and culinary values and the need to carefully manage the global population of herring. All are key to sustaining the world's herring populace.

Thus far Atlantic herring has benefited from these celebrations and renewed awareness. At present its future appears fairly stable. Habitat restoration has enabled depleted communities to bounce back and remain viable. In Maine efforts to restore fish passages or fishways, routes that fish such as sturgeon, shad and herring take to spawn, have yielded positive results. When dams are removed, new fishways are installed and the natural habitat is rebuilt, herring are able to travel freely, find food more easily and reproduce. According to a 2011 report from the National Oceanic and Atmospheric Administration, through restoration efforts the herring population around Augusta, Maine, climbed from almost zero in 1985 to three million by 2009. Other North Atlantic regions have likewise witnessed the fish's gradual but steady return.

Catch restrictions and improved fishery management have also allowed Atlantic herring to recover. The disastrous billion-pound hauls of the late 1960s have been replaced by more moderate annual catch limits of 200 million pounds (91 million kg). As a result, as of late 2015, Atlantic herring did not fall into the category of 'overfished'; it continues to be sustainably harvested. Its population is resilient enough to support the demands not only of other fish, birds and marine animals, but of man.

The outlook for Pacific herring remains more doubtful. Because of climate change, destruction of breeding and feeding grounds and overfishing, Pacific herring has seen its numbers dwindle dramatically. Through conservation efforts its situation is slowly improving, but the debate continues over whether the fish will regain its former abundance.

The hope is that through continued public education, sustainable fishing and thoughtful consumption, both Atlantic and Pacific herring will have bright outcomes. Rather than turn into relics of the past, they will become a healthful and renewable food choice for the future. If treated with the consideration and respect that these ancient fish deserve, herring will sustain mankind for generations to come.

Recipes

Basic Pickled Herring

2 pounds (910 g) skinless salted herring fillets
1 cup (240 ml) water, plus more for soaking the herring fillets
1 cup (240 ml) white wine vinegar
⅔ cup (135 g) sugar
1 tsp black peppercorns
½ tsp whole allspice
1 small yellow onion, sliced
2 bay leaves

Place the herring fillets in a large bowl filled with cold water. Refrigerate for 24 hours, changing the water twice during this time to reduce the saltiness of the fish.

To make the pickling liquid, put the water, vinegar, sugar, peppercorns and allspice in a large saucepan and bring to the boil over a medium-high heat. Once the solution has started to boil, remove the pan from the heat and allow it to cool slightly.

Rinse off and dry the herring fillets. Using a sharp knife, cut the fish into 2-inch (5-cm) pieces and remove any bones.

Put equal amounts of herring and onions with the bay leaves into lidded jars. Pour equal amounts of pickling solution over the fish and onions. Place the caps on the jars and refrigerate for a minimum of three days.

Makes 2 pints (950 ml)

Mustard-marinated Herring

When refrigerated, mustard-marinated herring will keep for one week.

2 ¼ pounds (1 kg) small herring fillets

For the first marinade:
2 cups (480 ml) water
1 ¼ cups (300 ml) white wine vinegar
1 tsp sea (Kosher) salt
1 tsp granulated sugar

For the second marinade:
3 tbsp wholegrain mustard
2 tbsp Dijon mustard
3 tbsp granulated sugar
1 tbsp firmly packed light brown sugar
1 small shallot, sliced
2 tsp sea (Kosher) salt
1 tsp black peppercorns
3 cups (720 ml) water
¼ cup (60 ml) cider vinegar
¼ cup (60 ml) grapeseed or rapeseed (canola) oil

Wash the herring fillets and lay them in a large, deep dish. Whisk together the water, vinegar, salt and sugar and pour it over the fish. Cover the dish with plastic wrap and refrigerate for eight hours.

While the fish is macerating, mix together the mustards, sugars, shallot, salt, peppercorns, water, vinegar and oil for the second marinade.

After eight hours, remove the herring from the marinade and dry off each fillet with a paper towel. Place the fillets on a cutting board and, using a sharp knife, slice each into 2-in. (5-cm) long and 1-in. (2.5-cm) wide strips.

Place the herring in another large, deep dish or bowl. Pour the mustard marinade over the top, cover and refrigerate for 24 hours, tossing the herring periodically so that all the slices are marinated equally.

After 24 hours remove the herring from the marinade and serve on rye bread.

Serves 8

Branteviks Herring

For the first marinade:
1 lb (450 g) skinless, salt-cured
herring fillets
1 cup (40 ml) white vinegar
6 tbsp water
1 tbsp salt

For the second marinade:
1 cup (200 g) granulated sugar
20 white peppercorns, crushed
20 whole allspice, crushed
1 large white onion, chopped
1 large red onion, chopped
1 tbsp grated lemon zest
1 tsp ground black pepper
1 bay leaf, crushed
1 small bundle of fresh dill, chopped

Soak the herring fillets in cold water for six hours, changing the water once or twice during this time. When finished, pat the fillets dry with a clean cloth.

For the first marinade, whisk together the vinegar, water and salt. Place the herring fillets in a shallow baking dish and pour the liquid over them. Cover and refrigerate for twelve hours or overnight.

Remove the dish from the refrigerator and drain the marinade into a bowl. Add the sugar, peppercorns, allspice, onions, lemon zest, ground pepper, bay leaf and dill and stir.

Alternating between layers of herring and marinade, fill a lidded glass jar or container with the fish. Make sure the herring is neatly packed and not floating about. You may need to drain off or withhold a bit of liquid. Don't skimp, though, on the onion, spice and herb mixture.

Seal and refrigerate the container for at least 24 hours or up to three days before serving.

Rollmops

6 fresh herring fillets
1 cup (240 ml) cider vinegar
1 tsp granulated sugar
1 tbsp olive oil
2 bay leaves
1 sprig fresh tarragon
1 tsp black peppercorns
1 tsp coriander seeds, crushed
1 medium white onion, sliced into thin rings
2 hard-boiled eggs, chopped, for garnish
handful of fresh dill, for garnish

Place the vinegar, sugar, oil, bay leaves, tarragon, peppercorns and coriander seeds in a non-reactive saucepan. Simmer, covered, for ten minutes. Remove from the heat and let cool.

Using a large, wide-mouthed jar or a deep, glass baking dish, arrange half the onions on the bottom. Cover them with three herring fillets. Pour half of the vinegar mixture over the fillets. Top with onions and herring and add the remaining vinegar mixture.

Cover the casserole or jar with plastic wrap and allow the herring to marinate in the refrigerator for at least two days or up to one week.

To serve the pickled herring fillets, drain and then arrange them on a platter. Garnish with hard-boiled eggs and dill and serve.

Serves 4 to 6

Chopped Herring

Originating in Eastern Europe, this Jewish speciality comes in countless variations. Some cooks make chopped herring with only herring and eggs or apples. Others include breadcrumbs, sugar, herbs or spices, along with the pickling liquid, vegetable oil or lemon juice. The following is the most commonly found recipe for chopped herring. Feel free to adapt depending on your taste and pantry supplies.

3 hard-boiled eggs
1 (16-oz or 450-g) jar pickled herring, drained
1 medium white onion, sliced
2 apples, peeled and sliced
juice of ½ lemon, optional

Dice one egg and set it aside. Place the remaining ingredients in the bowl of a food processor and pulse together until chopped. Spoon the chopped herring into a bowl, sprinkle the top with the diced egg, cover and refrigerate until ready to serve.
Serves 6

Pickled Beet and Herring Salad

Scandinavian in origin, this tart, cold salad is known in that region as *sillsallad*. Sour cream and sliced hard-boiled eggs often accompany this dish.

1 cup (230 g) pickled herring,
drained and diced
3 cups (800 g) cooked beetroot (beets),
chilled and diced
¼ cup (40 g) diced yellow onion
1 green apple, peeled and diced
2 tbsp minced flat-leaf parsley
3 tbsp cider vinegar

2 tbsp cold water
salt to taste
¼ tsp ground black pepper
2 tbsp freshly squeezed lemon juice
1 tsp granulated sugar
sour cream, optional, for serving

In a medium serving bowl mix together the herring, beetroot, onion and apple. In a separate bowl, whisk together the parsley, cider vinegar, water, salt and pepper and pour it over the salad. Cover and refrigerate until chilled.

Before serving, mix together the lemon juice and sugar. Drizzle over the salad and serve.

Serves 4 to 6

North Holland Salad

1 head butterhead lettuce, such as Boston or Bibb,
leaves separated and washed
1½ lb (680 g) firm, waxy potatoes, boiled and sliced
2 hard-boiled eggs, sliced
3.5 oz (100 g) Edam cheese, cut into
thin strips
4 pickled herring fillets, drained
3 tbsp olive oil
1 tbsp sherry vinegar
1 tbsp minced shallot
½ tsp salt
¼ tsp ground black pepper
¼ tsp Dijon mustard
4 sweet pickled gherkins, chopped
1 tsp capers, drained and rinsed

Spread the lettuce leaves on a serving platter. Place the sliced potatoes, followed by the eggs and strips of cheese, over the lettuce. Top these with the herring.

Whisk together the oil, vinegar, shallot, salt, pepper and mustard. Pour the dressing over the salad. Sprinkle the gherkins and capers over the top and serve.

Serves 2 to 4

Onion-herring Pissaladière

The flaky, rich tart known as pissaladière hails from Nice, France. There it features anchovies, onions and oil-cured black olives. Here pickled herring stand in for the anchovies, giving the pissaladière a lighter, slightly more complex flavour.

1 sheet of frozen puff pastry, thawed
3 tbsp (45 ml) olive oil
1½ medium white onions, halved and sliced into thin crescents
¾ tsp sea salt
4 oz (115 g) pickled herring, drained and rinsed
1 tsp chopped fresh rosemary
½ tsp dried thyme

Preheat the oven to 400°F/200°C. Roll out the thawed puff pastry to ¼-inch (½-cm) thick and place it on an ungreased baking sheet.

In a medium frying or sauté pan, heat the oil on medium high. Add the onions and salt and sauté until softened and slightly coloured, about six minutes. Remove the onions from the pan and spread them evenly over the puff pastry. Using your fingers, break the herring into chunks and place them on top of the onions, spacing them evenly apart. Sprinkle the fresh rosemary and dried thyme over the onions and herring and insert the pissaladière into the oven. Bake for fifteen to twenty minutes, until the pastry has puffed up and the edges have browned slightly. Cut into squares and serve warm.

Serves 4 to 6

Grilled Herring

1 tsp olive oil
4 fresh herrings, cleaned but left whole
sea salt, to taste
ground black pepper, to taste
soy sauce, optional, for serving
lemon juice, optional, for serving

(NB: what UK readers call a grill, Americans call a broiler.) Spread the olive oil over a sheet of aluminum foil and place the herring on top. Put the oven rack in the second slot from the top of the oven and preheat the grill on high.

Sprinkle the herring with salt and ground black pepper. Reduce the grill to medium, place the foil with the fish directly onto the rack and grill for fifteen minutes. Using tongs or a fish spatula, flip over the fish and sprinkle salt and pepper on the other side. Grill for another five to ten minutes, until the flesh is flaky when probed with a fork.

To serve, sprinkle soy sauce or lemon juice over the broiled herring or consume as is.

Serves 4

Scottish Fried Herring

For a truly traditional Scottish meal, fry twelve rashers of good-quality streaky bacon. After removing the bacon from the pan, cook the oat-coated herring in the leftover bacon fat. Serve the fish alongside the bacon.

1 cup (100 g) uncooked rolled oats
½ tsp sea salt, plus more for seasoning
½ tsp freshly ground black pepper, plus more
for seasoning
2 large eggs
2 tbsp water

6 large (generous 1 lb or 450 g) herrings, cleaned and deboned
2 oz (60 g) unsalted butter

Toss together the oats, salt and pepper. Spread the mixture on a plate. Whisk together the eggs and water.

Season the herring with salt and pepper. Dip the fish into the egg mixture, making sure that it is evenly coated before pressing it into the rolled oats. Repeat for the remaining herring and set aside.

Melt half the butter in a large frying pan over a medium heat. Add the herring and fry on one side until golden brown, two to three minutes. Add the remaining butter to the pan and gently turn over the herring. Cook on the other side until golden brown, two to three minutes. Remove from the pan and serve hot.
Serves 6

Lemon- and Herb-stuffed Herring

1 tbsp olive oil
sea salt, to taste
freshly ground black pepper, to taste
12 large (2 lb or 900 g) whole herrings, cleaned and deboned
¾ cup (85 g) dry breadcrumbs
3 tbsp grated Parmesan cheese
1 garlic clove, minced
¼ cup (4 tbsp) chopped, fresh flat-leaf parsley
1 tbsp minced fresh basil
grated zest of 1 lemon
1 tbsp freshly squeezed lemon juice
½ tsp sea salt
¼ tsp freshly ground black pepper
4 tbsp extra-virgin olive oil

Preheat the oven to 400°F/200°C. Grease the bottom of a large baking dish with olive oil. Season the herring with salt and pepper and then place them on their sides in the baking dish.

In a medium-sized bowl mix together the breadcrumbs, cheese, garlic, parsley, basil, lemon zest and juice, salt, pepper, and 2 tbsp extra-virgin olive oil. Taste and adjust the seasonings as needed.

Using your fingers or a spoon, spread equal amounts of stuffing inside each herring. Drizzle the remaining oil over the top of the herring. Bake until tender when probed with a fork, about fifteen minutes. Serve warm.

Serves 4 to 6

Smoked Herring Tea Sandwiches

Adapted from Kathy Hunt's *Fish Market* (Running Press, 2013)

While these make lovely canapés, you can also serve them as traditional, deli-style sandwiches. Simply assemble as you would a regular sandwich, leaving the bread slices whole, and pair alongside dill pickles.

8 slices fresh multi-grain bread, cut into quarters
2–3 oz (50–75 g) cream cheese, at room temperature
4–8 Bibb lettuce leaves, cut to fit the bread
4 large smoked herrings, cut into quarters
½ small red onion, thinly sliced
2 plum tomatoes, thinly sliced
dill pickles, optional, for serving

Taking a square of bread, spread a thin layer of cream cheese over one side. Place a piece of lettuce and then herring, followed by equal amounts of onion and tomato, on top of the bread. Spread a thin layer of cream cheese over another slice of bread and lay it, dressed-side down, on top of the sandwich filling. Repeat until you have sixteen sandwiches. Serve as is or with dill pickles.

Serves 4 to 6

Clay Pot Herring

¼ tsp freshly ground white pepper
¼ cup (30 g) dry breadcrumbs
2 tbsp grated Pecorino Romano cheese
2 tbsp (30 g) unsalted butter
2 small white onions, halved and thinly sliced
1½ lb (680 g) Idaho or Russet potatoes, peeled, halved and sliced
into ¼-in. (2-cm) thick crescents
4 oz (110 g) smoked herring, sliced into 2-in. (5-cm) pieces
¾ cup (180 ml) heavy (double) cream
½ cup (120 ml) whole milk
1 tbsp (15 g) salted butter, melted

Preheat the oven to 400°F/200°C. Grease a 2-quart (2-litre) baking dish. In a small bowl mix together the pepper, breadcrumbs, and cheese and set aside.

Melt the unsalted butter in a medium-sized frying or sauté pan on a medium heat. Add the onions and sauté until golden in colour, about seven minutes.

Place half of the potatoes in the bottom of the greased dish. Layer the onions, followed by the herring and remaining potatoes, over them. You may need to press down on the layers so that everything fits snugly in the dish.

Whisk together the cream and milk and pour it into the baking dish. Sprinkle the breadcrumb mixture over the potatoes and then drizzle the melted butter over the top. Bake for 45 minutes, until the potatoes are soft and golden brown. Serve warm.
Serves 4 to 6

Kazunoko

This traditional Japanese dish is a mainstay of Japanese New Year or *Osechi Riyōri* feasts. Along with bringing prosperity, the marinated herring eggs symbolize fertility in the coming year.

4 herring roes
3 cups (720 ml) water
½ cup (120 ml) dashi
1 ½ tbsp soy sauce
1 ½ tbsp mirin
dried bonito flakes, to serve

To reduce the roe's saltiness, place the roe and water in a large bowl, cover and refrigerate overnight.

To make the marinade, pour the dashi, soy sauce and mirin into a small saucepan and bring to a boil. Allow the liquids to simmer for one minute before removing the pan from the heat and let the ingredients cool to room temperature.

As the liquid is cooling, remove the roe from the refrigerator and drain off the water. Remove the white membrane surrounding the roe sacks and then slice the roe into 1-inch (2-cm) pieces. Put the roe slices in a clean bowl.

Once the marinade has cooled, pour it over the roe. Cover and refrigerate for a minimum of twelve hours so that the roe can marinate. To serve, mound the roe onto four plates and sprinkle each serving with dried bonito flakes.

Serves 4

Sautéed Herring Roe

Shad roe can also be prepared in this manner.

4 tbsp (60 g) unsalted butter
12 oz (340 g) herring roe
2 tbsp freshly squeezed lemon juice
sea salt, to taste
freshly ground white pepper, to taste

In a large non-stick skillet melt the butter on a medium heat. Swirl it around the pan before adding the roe. Cook the roe on one side until lightly browned, about three minutes. Turn over and allow the other side to brown. When finished, the roe should be golden brown in colour.

Remove the roe from the pan. Add the lemon juice to the remaining butter and whisk together. Pour the liquid over the roe and season with salt and white pepper, to taste.

Serves 4

Select Bibliography

Arthur, Michael Samuel, *The Herring: Its Effects on the History of Britain* (London, 1918)

Colquhoun, Kate, *Taste* (New York, 2007)

Cook, Joseph J., *The Incredible Atlantic Herring* (New York, 1979)

Cumming, Joseph George, *The Isle of Man* (London, 1861)

Davidson, Alan, *Oxford Companion to Food* (Oxford, 2008)

De Moor, Janny, *Dutch Cooking* (London, 2007)

Food and Agriculture Organization of the United Nations, Fisheries Division, 'Herring and Allied Species: A Commodity Study 1928–48' (Washington, DC, 1949)

Green, Aliza, *Field Guide to Seafood* (Philadelphia, PA, 2007)

Grigson, Jane, *Jane Grigson's Fish Book* (London, 1993)

Hix, Mark, *British Regional Food* (London, 2006)

Hodgson, W. C., *The Herring and Its Fishery* (London, 1957)

Howell, David Luke, *Capitalism from Within: Economy, Society and the State in a Japanese Fishery* (Oakland, CA, 1995)

Hybel, Nils, and Bjorn Poulsen, *The Danish Resources, c. 1000–1550: Growth and Recession* (Leiden, 2007)

Jesch, Judith, ed., *The Scandinavians from the Vendel Period to the Tenth Century* (San Marino, 2002)

Johnson, Ruth A., *All Things Medieval* (Santa Barbara, CA, 2011)

Langdon, Frank, *The Politics of Canadian-Japanese Economic Relations, 1952–1983* (Vancouver, 1983)

Larousse Gastronomique: The World's Greatest Culinary Encyclopedia (New York, 2009)

Maddigan, Michael J., *Nemasket River Herring: A History* (Charleston, NC, 2014)

Mariani, John, *Encyclopedia of American Food and Drink* (New York, 1999)

McCormick Smith, Hugh, *King Herring* (Washington, DC, 1909)

Mitchell, John, *The Herring: Its Natural History and National Importance* (Edinburgh, 1864)

Mortimer, Ian, *The Time Traveler's Guide to Medieval England* (New York, 2011)

Munro, R. J., *The Herring Fisheries* (London, 1884)

Murray, Donald S., *Herring Tales* (London, 2015)

Plum, Camilla, *The Scandinavian Kitchen* (London, 2011)

Preger, W., *The Humble Dutch Herring* (Melbourne, 1944)

Price, Bill, *Fifty Foods that Changed the Course of History* (London, 2014)

Pulsiano, Phillip, and Kirstean Wolf, eds, *Medieval Scandinavia: An Encyclopedia* (New York, 1993)

Rick, Torben C., and Jon Erlandson, *Human Impacts on Ancient Marine Ecosystems* (Oakland, CA, 2008)

Root, Waverley, *Food* (New York, 1980)

Smylie, Mike, *Herring: A History of the Silver Darlings* (Stroud, 2006)

Toussaint-Samat, Maguelonne, *A History of Food* (Hoboken, NJ, 2008)

Triberg, Annica, *Very Swedish* (Stockholm, 2007)

Van Waerebeek, Ruth, *Everybody Eats Well in Belgium Cookbook* (New York, 1996)

Whiteman, Kate, *The World Encyclopedia of Fish and Shellfish* (London, 2010)

Yeatman, Marwood, *The Last Food of England* (London, 2007)

Websites and Associations

Atlantic States Marine Fisheries Commission
www.asmfc.org

California Department of Fish and Wildlife
www.dfg.ca.gov

Environmental Defense Fund
https://edf.org

Exxon Valdez Oil Spill Trustee Council
www.evostc.state.ak.us/index.cfm?FA=status.herring

The Fish Site
www.thefishsite.com/
articles/1288production-consumption-of-fishmeal

Gulf of Maine Research Institute
www.gma.org/herring

Hatchery International
hatcheryinternational.com/restocking/japan's-herring-
hatcheries

Herring Era Museum
www.sild.is/en/history/history-in-short/nr/142

NOAA Fish Watch Atlantic Herring
www.fishwatch.gov/profiles/atlantic-herring

Pacific Herring
www.pacificherring.org

Terra Scaniae
http://archive.is/20130418132720/www.ts.skane.se/fakta/
skaanemarknaden

Acknowledgements

First and foremost, I must thank publisher Michael Leaman of Reaktion Books and Edible series editor Andrew F. Smith for allowing me to write this book. Thanks to their generosity, I can share my fascination with herring and educate others about this historic, little fish.

No writer creates a work of non-fiction without some help and encouragement. To wit, I am indebted to the staff of the New York Public Library's Stephen A. Schwarzman Building and General Research Division. Their unending patience and time-liness with my innumerable requests made researching a breeze.

Likewise, I am grateful for the assistance of Maria Groes Eldh of Skagen Turisthus Nord in Skagen, Denmark. Without Maria I would not have attended the early morning Skagen fish auctions, experienced fresh-from-the-boat herring or witnessed Scandinavian fishermen in action. These experiences proved invaluable in the writing of *Herring*.

Credit is likewise due to Gilad Langer for sharing his know-ledge of herring. He graciously participated in repeated conversa-tions and correspondence about how Danes cook and eat this fish.

Many friends aided in this project. Rachael Bankes and Zach Vanderveen provided first-hand accounts of kayaking with herring, while Christina Anderson introduced me to that unique Swedish delicacy *surströmming*. Elizabeth Theisen, Jane Wilmer, Marilee Morrow, Nickie Kolovos and Susan Havison provided gentle nudges and enquiries about my progress with this book. As always, I appreciate their and all other friends' insights and encouragement.

Few people would jump at the chance to spend their pre-dawn hours at Japanese, Scandinavian and Eastern European fish markets. That my husband Sean Dippold does so with good humour – far better humour than I possess at 4 a.m. – is a godsend. I am thankful for his eagerness to travel the globe with me in search of exotic foods and adventures. I am even more grateful for his unending support.

Without the late William G. Hunt as my father I may never have developed an interest in seafood. He was one of the earliest shapers of my palate and desire to try different cuisines. In adulthood Frank Wilmer played a similarly important role. Friend, fellow foodie, fishing buddy, literature lover and unwitting mentor, Frank unexpectedly passed away before this book was published. As with my father, Frank's spirit will live on through my love of writing, travel, history and food. I dedicate *Herring* to him.

Photo Acknowledgements

The author and the publishers wish to express their thanks to the below sources of illustrative material and/or permission to reproduce it.

タクナワン: p. 87; Alamy: p. 6 (Chris Wilson); Deseronto Archives: p. 76; Kathy Hunt: pp. 11, 13, 18, 30, 32, 36, 38, 44, 49, 53, 57, 61, 62, 86, 98, 108, 110, 113, 115; Library of Congress, Washington, DC: pp. 26, 27, 34, 42; LSE Library: p. 66; National Archives of the Netherlands – Nationaal Archief: pp. 12, 43; National Library of Norway: p. 39; Newcastle Libraries: pp. 67, 68; Oddman47: p. 102; OpenCage: p. 16; Prankster: p. 51; Swedish National Heritage Board: p. 24; UBC Library: p. 29; USFWS: p. 28; U.S. National Oceanic and Atmospheric Administration (NOAA): pp. 19 (Gulf of the Farallones NMS), 31 (Robert K. Brigham), 100 (NOAA's Historic Fisheries Collection), 105.

Index

italic numbers refer to illustrations; **bold** to recipes